Postmodern Vernaculars

PETER LANG
New York • Washington, D.C./Baltimore • Bern
Frankfurt am Main • Berlin • Brussels • Vienna • Oxford

Elisabeth Mermann-Jozwiak

Postmodern Vernaculars

Chicana Literature and Postmodern Rhetoric

PETER LANG
New York • Washington, D.C./Baltimore • Bern
Frankfurt am Main • Berlin • Brussels • Vienna • Oxford

Library of Congress Cataloging-in-Publication Data

Mermann-Jozwiak, Elisabeth.
Postmodern vernaculars: Chicana literature and postmodern rhetoric /
Elisabeth Mermann-Jozwiak.
p. cm.
Includes bibliographical references and index.
1. American literature—Mexican American authors—History and criticism.
2. English language—United States—Rhetoric. 3. Mexican American women—
Intellectual life. 4. Postmodernism (Literature)—United States.
5. Mexican American women in literature. I. Title.
PS153.M4M364   810.9'86872—dc22   2004027487
ISBN 0-8204-7634-X

Bibliographic information published by **Die Deutsche Bibliothek**.
Die Deutsche Bibliothek lists this publication in the "Deutsche
Nationalbibliografie"; detailed bibliographic data is available
on the Internet at http://dnb.ddb.de/.

Cover design by Lisa Barfield

The paper in this book meets the guidelines for permanence and durability
of the Committee on Production Guidelines for Book Longevity
of the Council of Library Resources.

© 2005 Peter Lang Publishing, Inc., New York
275 Seventh Avenue, 28th Floor, New York, NY 10001
www.peterlangusa.com

Printed in the United States of America

Contents

Acknowledgments

This book is the product of several years' work. At Texas A&M University in Corpus Christi, I've found a supportive community that encouraged me to go forward with this project. Many thanks to my colleagues and friends for putting up with my obsessions. First, to my team-teaching partner and collaborator, Nancy M. Sullivan, who taught me to see linguistics from an entirely new perspective, and whose work on language attitudes has influenced my own. For their careful reading of drafts and comments that challenged me to think through my arguments more clearly, I thank my readers and critics from the Departments of English and Humanities, Glenn Blalock, Diana Cardenas, Catherine Cox, Janis Haswell, Vanessa Jackson, Cristina Kirklighter, Susan Loudermilk, Anthony Quiroz, and Sharon Talley. I am grateful to Liliana Castañeda-Rossmann, with whom I enjoyed *Kaffeestunde* and conversations on things postmodern. For the many learning experiences they've provided me with, I thank the students in my Chicana literature courses, especially Marti Flores, Lara Hooper, Leah Jackson, Sofi Longoria, and Sandra Valerio. I gratefully acknowledge the financial support of several Texas A&M University-Corpus Christi Organized Research grants, as well as College of Arts and Humanities grants that have allowed me to draft significant portions of the manuscript. For their assistance in locating documents, I thank the Special Collections staff at Bell Library, especially Thomas Kreneck. This work has also benefitted from provocative comments from the audiences at the Narrative and Twentieth-Century Literature Conferences; thanks especially to Marianne deKoven and Susan Stanford Friedman.

Above all, my work would not have been possible without Joe, my first reader, critic *par excellence*, and partner in life. I am grateful for his readings, critical discussion, technological know-how, and extreme patience. Thanks for inviting me to relax from time to time. Andreas and Daniel, thank you for letting me get on board with you to discover new places and destinations. This book is dedicated to Theo and Maria Mermann, who first allowed me to explore new places.

permission from the publisher of *Chants* (Houston: Arte Público Press– University of Houston, 1985). "Bilingual Christmas," "Echoes," "Sonrisas," and "Unnatural Speech" by Pat Mora are reprinted with permission from the publisher of *Borders* (Houston: Arte Público Press–University of Houston, 1986). "Para un Revolucionario" by Lorna Dee Cervantes is reprinted with permission from the publisher of *The Americas Review* (Houston: Arte Público Press–University of Houston, 1975). Portions of chapter two are reprinted with permission from *Modern Fiction Studies,* 50.2 (Summer 2004). Portions of chapter four are reprinted with permission from *MELUS*, 25.2 (2000). The photograph in figure 1 is reprinted with permission from The Associated Press. Thanks to Lara Hooper and Joseph Jozwiak for allowing me to reprint their photographs (figures 2 and 3).

Introduction:
Toward a Chicana Postmodernism

In the mid– to late 1980s, Chicana authors were becoming more and more visible on the U.S. publishing scene. The decade, which ironically also saw proclamations of the demise of postmodernism, witnessed landmark publications of works by Gloria Anzaldúa, Sandra Cisneros, Ana Castillo, and others, many of whom now publish with major presses. Their works characteristically are highly experimental: their hybrid narratives; their fusion of prose and poetry, autobiography and essay, myth and history; and their blending of English and Spanish attest to the innovative nature of these texts. In an interview Cisneros, for example, has said: "I'm just not taken by the linear novel form . . . I'm much more interested in something new happening to the literature" (Dasenbrook and Jussawalla 304). Such intersections suggest the necessity for a close examination of the relationship between Chicana literature and theories of postmodernism. This study aligns Chicana texts with postmodernism, two traditions frequently seen as fundamentally incompatible, fraught with conflict, permeated by issues of power and domination, and arising from very different social and theoretical sites of enunciation. The one, Chicana literature, is inextricably tied to the social, cultural, and historical context of the Chicano/a movement. The other, postmodernism, is a Euro-centric phenomenon often characterized as rather ahistorical and apolitical.

This introduction will map the theoretical foundations for a dialogue between Chicana literature and postmodern theory. I begin by outlining the Chicano movement and the role of Chicanas within that movement. I then trace the evolution of postmodern theory to develop the concept of postmodern vernaculars. My argument is that postmodernism is not a monolithic phenomenon but one that is multiple and diverse. Finally, through an analysis of works by Alicia Gaspar de Alba and Emma Pérez, I show how Chicana literature is one vernacular of postmodernism.

The Chicano movement came into existence within the context of the Black

Civil Rights and Black Power movements in the late 1960s and 1970s.[1] It sought
to address the Mexican American community's social and economic inequalities
in American society. Serving as an umbrella for the diverse issues Mexican
Americans faced, the movement aimed to achieve social justice on a broad scale.
In New Mexico, the land grant movement led by Reies López Tijerina called for
the return of the land to the dispossessed hispanos. In California, Cesar Chávez
and Dolores Huerta were instrumental in the unionization of workers (National
Farm Workers' Association) and led the 1965 grape pickers' strike for increased
pay and standard working conditions in Delano. In the same year, Rodolfo
"Corky" Gonzales founded the Crusade for Justice in Denver, which protested
against poverty, poor housing conditions, and discrimination against Mexican
Americans. In Texas, the movement led to the foundation of a third political party,
the Raza Unida Party, which challenged the state's political system for its
systematic exclusion of Mexican Americans. Another concern was creating
educational opportunities; leaders organized school boycotts and aided in the
development of Chicano Studies programs on various college campuses in the
southwestern United States.

At the same time as the movement demanded equal rights for Mexican
Americans, it had a separatist and nationalist agenda as well. It advocated unity and
national consciousness among Chicanos and issued calls for self-determination.
Indicative of this endeavor was the "Plan Espiritual de Aztlán," produced at the
Denver Chicano Youth Liberation Conference in 1969, organized by the Crusade
for Justice. It begins with words that proclaim the dawning of a new era: "In the
spirit of a new people that is conscious not only of its proud historical heritage, but
also of the brutal 'gringo' invasion of our territories . . ." (Valdez and Steiner
402–3), and continues with a declaration of independence from European
American domination as well as an attempt to reclaim Aztlán, the mythical
homeland of the Chicano people. The plan was crucial in shaping the discourse of
Chicano ethnic consciousness.

The movement also sparked a renaissance of Mexican American literature that
expressed the experiences of Chicanos. José Antonio Villarreal's novel *Pocho* (1959)
was hailed as the first work of Chicano prose fiction, and Tomás Rivera's short
stories were widely distributed. Poets such as Alurista and José Montoya began to
publish their works. Playwright Luis Valdez founded the Teatro Campesino and
wrote his Actos, one-act plays performed by and for farm workers. This era also
saw the founding of journals such as *Quinto Sol* and *El Grito*. These literary projects

were driven by the need for an affirmation of identity, an emphasis on collective consciousness, a desire for self-determination, and a need to validate Mexican history, mythology, and folklore.

The discourse of Chicano nationalism is evident in social activist/writer Gonzales's "I am Joaquín: Yo soy Joaquín" (1967). The poem celebrates Chicano identity but intricately connects that identity to a masculinity that leaves virtually no room for female experiences. It begins by outlining the speaker's condition of confusion as he is "caught up in the whirl of a gringo society." He develops a selfhood through a series of identifications with historical and mythical figures, including Cuauhtémoc, the Aztec warrior killed by Cortés; Nezahualcóyotl, leader of the Chichimecas; and Pancho Villa, Mexican revolutionary leader, all prefaced by "I am" in analogy to the poem's title and first line. Women found themselves subsumed into a universal category of ethnic identity in many other works as well.[2] Angie Chabram-Dernersesian, writing about Armando B. Rendón's *Chicano Manifesto* (1971), argues that the book "reinforces dominant ideology by identifying machismo as the symbolic principle of Chicano revolt" (83). The effect of this was a silencing and removal of Chicanas' participation from the movement. In her poem "Para un Revolucionario," Lorna Dee Cervantes addresses her revolutionary brethren and points out the discrepancies between the men and the women of the movement. While the former speak of lofty ideals, the speaker remarks, "your voice is lost to me, carnal,/in the wail of tus hijos,/in the clatter of dishes/and the pucker of beans upon the stove" (151).

Building on a historical tradition of political activism on the part of immigrant Mexican women, Alma M. García writes, "Chicana feminists produced an ideological critique of the Chicano cultural nationalist movement that struggled against social injustice yet maintained patriarchal structures of domination" (1). They did so through a radical critique of patriarchal structures and a call for inclusion in the movement leadership.[3] But this critique also encompassed a re-visioning of some of the icons of Mexican American womanhood such as the Virgen de Guadalupe, emblematic of self-negation and self-sacrifice; La Malinche/Malintzín, the traitor of the Mexican people since she delivered them to Cortés; and la llorona, the weeping woman who drowned her children. Literary and visual artists revised such negative images and incorporated their experiences into the movement literature.[4]

Such appropriation and resignification, as well as parody, code-switching, and generic hybridity resulted in highly innovative texts to the extent that the postmodern rhetoric of the dissolution of boundaries, fluidity of identity, and bridging of opposites clearly seems to apply to many works by Chicana authors. However, I suggest that the current stage of intersection between postmodernism and Chicana literature is a long way away from early formulations of the postmodern, and indicative of the transformations the theory itself has undergone. Postmodern theory today, I would argue, is more complex than its detractors make it seem. Its development, from the 1960s and 70s through the 1980s and 90s, has shown postmodern theory as changing, diverse, and multiple. To account for this heterogeneity, I propose the notion of "postmodern vernaculars"—varieties of postmodernism that exist synchronically and diachronically and that yield significant variations to the "standard" language of critical studies—what I call "high postmodernism." "High postmodernism" is a theoretical construct that gained prominence in the academy in the 1960s and early 70s, and that monologically defined postmodern practices as radical experimentation with form and language. Such constructs have long been seen as the dominant articulations of the postmodern and have led to the canonization of radically experimental writers such as John Barth, Raymond Federman, and Thomas Pynchon, and to the exclusion of women and people of color.

The image of postmodernism in both academic discourses and in the popular imagination has long been one of elitist "*art pour art*." Theoretical discussions frequently focus on formal and linguistic experimentation, and studies as diverse as those by Brian McHale and Ellen G. Friedman and Miriam Fuchs all identify a list of techniques, including pastiche, briccolage, appropriation, and misappropriation as defining features of postmodernism.[5] Frederick Barthelme adequately captures this mode of self-reflexivity when he describes early postmodern literature as arguments about language dressed up as fiction. He explains, "The post-modernism of the 1960s and 70s . . . was like getting a snapshot of the town and then making a lot of jokes about it. This as a means of coming to know something was, if not the town, then just as good as the town" (26).

Such definitions of postmodernism as aesthetic practice maintain the form/content dichotomy characteristic of discourses on modern art and the avant-garde, separating politics from aesthetics.[6] Hence Fredric Jameson speaks of a depletion of content and exclusive focus on surfaces that lead to an "historical amnesia" affecting postmodernism ("Postmodernism" 125), a comment echoed in a *New York Times Book Review* article by sociologist Todd Gitlin. Gitlin claims that postmodernism "neither embraces nor critiques but beholds the world blankly" (35). According to Barthelme, Gitlin, and, more recently, Miriam Marty Clark, who argues in an essay on the postmodern short story that "the story becomes a logical vehicle for the displacement of postmodern loss and the thematization of diminished, even failing historicity" (153), postmodern artists assume an attitude of detachment, irony, and ambiguity. Similarly, Andy Grundberg, when he jubilantly but prematurely proclaims the demise of postmodernism, characterizes postmodern works as lacking historical consciousness as well as spiritual and social values due to their engagement with popular culture: "So many artists have borrowed their images from popular culture that appropriation and pastiche seem old hat." He concludes, "the future belongs to those artists who have no doubt about the righteousness of their positions and whose fields of reference are defined in indelible strokes" (52). Two assumptions guide this argument: first, that artists' engagement with history is inherently *not* postmodern; and second, that engagement with TV culture is inherently *not* political, an assessment that has been challenged by discussions within the field of cultural studies.

In these early formulations, works that present extreme formalist experimentation as Raymond Federman's and Marvin Cohen's are celebrated as high postmodern achievements while works by women or multicultural artists are conspicuously absent in discussions of metafiction, surfiction, or the narcissistic novel. In his list of "significant postmodern artists," all of whom are male, Jameson mentions Ishmael Reed as the only person of color ("Postmodernism" 118). Molly Hite's essay in *The Columbia History of the American Novel* mentions only two women, Kathy Acker and Joanna Russ, and two African American males (Reed and Samuel Delaney). Feminist revisionist narratives of postmodernism such as Marlene S. Barr's *Feminist Fabulations*, Patricia Waugh's *Feminine Fictions*, and Magali Cornier Michael's *Feminism and the Postmodern Impulse*, focus exclusively on works by white women writers.

However, at least since 1984, when Andreas Huyssen famously wrote that "women and minority artists . . . added a whole new dimension to the critique of high modernism and alternative forms of culture" (250), critics have interrogated constructions of such aesthetic and ahistorical postmodernism. Frederick R. Karl's comments that "Postmodernism and even Modernism have not yet entered into female discussions of the feminine experience" (424) make clear the enduring perception that women's writing is experiential (and therefore based on traditional models of narrative), and men's experimental. However, following Huyssen, theorists such as Linda Hutcheon and Ihab Hassan, in his later work, have sought to reconnect postmodernism to history and have linked postmodernism to postmodernity's critique of humanism and positivism. Hutcheon's focus on historical metafictions, for instance, illustrates that both feminism and multiculturalism "have worked to reconnect the ideological and the aesthetic" (*Poetics* 195). These critics have found it more helpful to link postmodernism to poststructuralism and define it as a Foucauldian episteme, an era whose main expression is a crisis of modernity—of Enlightenment narratives, unity, progress, representation, identities, and binary thinking of center and periphery.[7] Postmodernity, then, presents a rupture that is tied to social and economic developments in the Western world—the ascendancy of global capitalism, postindustrialism (Hoeveler), a mass society (Howe), "the cultural logic of late capitalism" (Jameson), and "scattered hegemonies," the effects of mobile capital and multiple subjectivities that replace the European unitary subject (Grewal and Kaplan 7).

Postmodernism, in this view, becomes a cultural response to conditions of postmodernity. For Jameson, whose focus on aesthetic postmodernism blinds him to the possibilities of a postmodernism of resistance, postmodernism represents "the internal and susperstructural expression of a whole new wave of American military and economic domination throughout the world: in this sense, as throughout class history, the underside of culture is blood, torture, death, and terror" ("Cultural Logic" 5). Within the context of critiques of modernity and in contrast to an exclusive focus on formal experimentation in much criticism on postmodernism, I suggest that postmodern practices engage in a cultural politics that expose the constructed nature of literary and social conventions. In the words of Hal Foster, "postmodernism is concerned with a critical deconstruction of tradition, not an instrumental pastiche of pop or pseudo- historical forms, with a critique of origins, not a return to them. In short, it seeks to question rather than exploit cultural codes, to explore rather than conceal social and political affiliations" (xii).

This study seeks to contribute to what I regard as a third-stage postmodernism, a theoretical manifestation that coexists with rather than supersedes the ones discussed previously, and one that broadens the debate. Characteristic of this stage is an attempt to establish links between diasporic U.S. literature and postmodernism. In the 1990s critics began to argue more vocally that multicultural and feminist theories and practices are central in theorizing a changing notion of the postmodern. This changing notion is contemporaneous, it is worth noting, with persisting definitions of the postmodern based on what I call high postmodernism. At national conferences in 2001, for example, despite Huyssen's proclaimed inclusion of "work by women and minorities," panels reveal that traditional notions of the postmodern are alive and well. For instance, at the 2001 Twentieth-Century Literature Conference, the canon of postmodernism was reiterated in panels such as Theorizing the Postmodern, Postmodernism and History, and Postmodern Fiction, with presenters discussing the works of Martin Amis, Paul Auster, Nicholson Baker, John Barth, Angela Carter, Bret Easton Ellis, John Garner, Don DeLillo, Gregory Maguire, and D.M. Thomas. Two panels were exclusively devoted to the works of Thomas Pynchon. Contributions that explored intersections were relegated to Ethnic Literature panels, a strategy that does not allow for much dialogue.[8] More productive have been examinations by W. Lawrence Hogue, for example, who has linked Asian American, African American, and Native American works of fiction to postmodernity and confirms the presence of a new postmodernism (18). Similarly, Phillip Brian Harper, Aldon Lynn Nielsen, and Rafael Pérez-Torres ("Between Presence") focus on contemporary African American literature and find resistant and critical postmodernism in these works, a postmodernism that gives rise to syncretism and hybridity and that crosses cultural and economic boundaries. Indicative of this shift in postmodern discourses is Tim Woods's *Beginning Postmodernism*, an introductory overview that reflects some of these changes and specifically addresses intersections among postmodernism and feminism, and postmodernism and postcolonialism.

While theorists of postmodernism have yet to acknowledge the experimental works by people of color, and "Chicano critical discourse," in the words of Angie Chabram, "has remained largely peripheral to greater critical developments" (146), many in the Chicano/a critical community have indeed recognized intersections with postmodernism. Chicano critics such as Pérez-Torres, Yvonne Yarbro-Bejarano, and others have related the experimentalism of Chicana texts to the social and historical context, and have viewed Chicana cultural production as instances of discursive resistance against dominant ideologies. Norma Alarcón, for instance, has indicated that Chicano works engage in textual politics or "revisionary dialogue" with older forms of representation ("The Sardonic Powers" 99). Similarly, Pérez-Torres describes the counter-discursivity of Chicana texts as "writ[ing] through and against, not in place of, dominant and dominating discourses" (*Movements* 34). As a result, again in Alarcón's words, "a variety of discourses can be negated, supplemented, modified, and repeated" (99). Moreover, Alvina Quintana has noted that Chicanas' "marginal position between ideologies contributes to new aesthetic opportunities, as it provides the writers with the strategic position to enhance or refute two outside sources and thereby contribute to the emergence of a new culture" ("Politics" 259).[9]

Pérez-Torres's book-length study *Movements in Chicano Poetry* explicitly argues for the need of multiculturalism to engage with postmodernism (226). Pérez-Torres characterizes Chicano culture as quintessentially postmodern, moving "both through the gaps and across the bridges between numerous cultural sites, the United States, Mexico, Texas, California, the rural, the urban, the folkloric, the postmodern, the popular, the elite, the traditional, the tendentious, the avant-garde" (3). Underlying these postmodern border crossings is a series of real historical ruptures and displacements. Chicano culture is, in this view, migratory, a term that "while evoking a history of actual displacement and economic exploitation . . . becomes a metaphor characterizing the movement between fixed cultural sites" (151).

While Pérez-Torres explicitly brings the two traditions together, other critics more casually label Chicano/a texts "postmodern" without theoretical reflection as to a possible dialogue between them. For example, Quintana and María Elena de Valdés unselfconsciously characterize Ana Castillo's *Mixquiahuala Letters* and Sandra Cisneros's *House on Mango Street*, respectively, as postmodern works (Quintana, *Home Girls* 80; Valdés 287). Similarly, Hector Calderón reads, without further comment, Tomás Rivera's *Y no se lo tragó la tierra* "as a Chicano version of a Third World postmodernism evident, for example, in Latin American and African literature" ("The Novel" 113). Moreover, Chicano/a critics frequently focus on discursive convergences with postmodernism, including its use of appropriation and pastiche, rupture, duplicity, and polyglossia (Pérez-Torres, *Movements*); schizophrenia, self-reflexivity, and generic hybridization (Tey Diana Rebolledo and Eliana S. Rivero, "Introduction"); and decentered subjectivity (Guillermo Gómez-Peña). The present study identifies specific overlapping tropes and discourses of borders, spaces, realism, genre, and language. By placing the traditions of postmodernism/poststructuralism and Chicana literature in a dialogue, it seeks to conduct a sustained examination of epistemic intersections

Nonetheless, there is still much resistance and skepticism on the part of Chicanos/as regarding such an alliance, and in Jameson's model of postmodern positions, many would find themselves in the anti-postmodern camp.[10] They respond to the theoretical implications of various aspects of postmodern theory—its ahistoricity, for example, its construction of subjectivity, or its denial of agency—and tend to react to a static concept of postmodernism as Euro-centric and concerned mainly with textuality. For instance, Raymond Rocco argues that one of the main shortcomings of postmodernism is its lack of historicity, its failure to account for race and class and, specifically, otherness (327). Along the same lines, Calderón and José Davíd Saldívar warn not to forget the historical ruptures underlying postmodern experimentation. They write that "any glossy version of a postmodern, postindustrial 'America' must be reinterpreted against the influx of Third World immigrants and the rapid re-Hispanicization of important regional sectors of our Mexican America and the wider United States" ("Editors' Introduction" 7). Similarly, Rebolledo rejects the (poststructuralist) death of the subject as not relevant to Chicano/a concerns and states, "postmodernism can only be approached in Chicano literature as an acknowledgment of multiple points of view on the part of writers and critics" (*Women* 4).

Many Chicano/a critics have rejected postmodernism's anti-foundationalism and ahistoricism as ineffective for a literature concerned with social change. In an influential 1987 article, "Postmodernism and Chicana Literature," Rosaura Sánchez, like Jameson, objects to the superficiality and "reduction of history and knowledge to textuality (4)."[11] She argues that "as long as the realm of the non-discursive is as important as the discursive level, as long as the literature continues to be marginal and deterritorialized, Chicano/a literature, albeit within the cultural dominant of postmodernism, will only be tangentially postmodern" (12). Instead, Chicano literature lies in "a heterogeneous literary space, as much modernist as pre-modernist" (7). While acknowledging Chicano writers' uses of some postmodern strategies, such as magic realism and parody, it is precisely this reduction of the postmodern to technique that betrays Sánchez's monolithic construction of the term and her adoption of Jameson's critique. Theoretically, she argues, Chicano and Chicana writers remain anti-postmodern in their frequent use of essentialist discourses where being Chicano is the defining difference that constitutes identity. This claim of a continued preoccupation with the unitary subject certainly is in large measure dependent on Sánchez's selection of authors. By no means do I wish to suggest that all Chicano/a literature is postmodern, but as I will show in the last part of this chapter, Chicana authors have participated in the depiction of the non-unitary subject, which they critique as a bourgeois construction.[12]

In 1999 Rosaura Sánchez reiterates and sharpens her assessment of postmodernism in an essay co-authored with Beatrice Pita. The authors argue that "minority literature in the U.S. and Third World literature in general grasped and inserted within the network of cultural commodity circulation and classified as postmodern examples of 'difference' . . . results in an uncomfortable fit" (309). They raise the important issue of the translatability of Euro-centric paradigms into different contexts in their assertion of postmodernism's inability to theorize class issues.[13] Sánchez and Pita arrive at this conclusion through an examination of works by Third World intellectuals produced between 1989–94, among whom they find widespread and uncritical acceptance of postmodernism and new social movement theories. In the authors' view, this demonstrates theorists' disconnection from workers in their countries. Instead of local and micro-level approaches to social change, which these intellectuals, in postmodern fashion, advocate, Sánchez and Pita stress the continued importance, in a Latin American context, of (Marxist) master narratives. Overall, the authors find an inherent incompatibility of Third World reality and Western theory to the point that Marxism/postmodernism becomes a static binary.[14]

From a different perspective, but driven by a similar concern for Chicana feminist politics, Paula M.L. Moya argues that postmodernism has replaced a "politics of liberation" with a "politics of difference." In the process, she critiques what she calls a pragmatist feminist theory as practiced by Norma Alarcón and Chela Sandoval, which encompasses an eclectic use of postmodernism and the "strategic" recourse to foundationalist (i.e., realist and identity-related) assumptions they endorse. These critics, she argues, by advocating a non-unitary subject and expanding the definition of "differential consciousness" (Sandoval) into an all-inclusive category, skate on relativism and ultimately undermine their own projects. Instead, Moya introduces a post-positivist framework, which propagates a belief in objective reality and views the world as not exclusively socially constructed. Rather, such a framework affirms that successive approximations of reality are indeed possible.

In contrast to Sánchez, Sánchez and Pita, Moya, and others critical of connections, I argue that it is necessary to revisit this supposed disjunction. These critics see an unbridgeable gap between Chicana literature and postmodernism resulting from a monolithic concept of the postmodern. The contemporaneous appearance of Chicana literature and postmodernism, as well as the empirical evidence of numerous discursive convergences, suggest the necessity for a reevaluation. Part of such reevaluation entails a move away from viewing postmodernism as static and unchanging, and acknowledging the transformative potential of theory. I outlined above some of the changes in postmodern theorizing from the 1960s to the present. In the discussions that follow in chapters one through five, I will show what effects Chicana literature can have on the postmodern. I argue that they can lead to new formulations of the postmodern, new insights on the periodization, and a broadened dialogue between the traditions.

In his defense against claims that using continental structuralist and poststructuralist theory is "antiblack," Henry Louis Gates, while realizing the risk of African American literature's enslavement to these methods (349), develops a more fluid notion of theory. He states, "I have tried to work through contemporary theories of literature *not* to 'apply' them to black texts, but rather to *transform* by *translating* them into a new rhetorical realm." This critical activity, he argues, is important to "sustain a truly comparative and pluralistic notion of the institution of literature" (351). His notion of theory, which derives from the Derridean concept of translation, according to which the critic transforms the theory by virtue of translating it into a different context, serves to "recreate, through revision, the critical theory at hand" (352). Chicano/a critics have similarly recognized this potential and, as Chabram demonstrates, significantly revise mainstream theories in a process of "appropriation and adaptation, where critical theories are constituted and reconstituted—often completely transformed—by virtue of their accommodation to the exigencies of new and distinct textual and cultural milieus" (138). As theory travels from one context to another, new versions are articulated, old ones enriched, supplemented, or abandoned.

Such a view can lead to a more positive assessment of the intersections among postmodernism and multicultural literature, as is evident in Chela Sandoval's work. Sandoval most clearly and emphatically aligns Third World women's work with postmodernism in her conceptualization of oppositional consciousness. She introduces the category of differential consciousness, a practice enacted by U.S. Third World Feminists that reflects the mobility and flexibility of the postmodern subject. These subjects have been forced to experience the aesthetics of a "postmodernism" as a requisite for survival (50). This aesthetics includes a "kinetic motion that maneuvers, poetically transfigures, and orchestrates while demanding alienation, perversion, and reformation in both spectators and practitioners" (3).

Such theoretization is useful in that it leads us to rethink postmodernism's periodization. It clearly suggests that there was a Third World women's postmodernism *avant la lettre*. Along similar lines, performance artist Guillermo Gómez-Peña has stated about Chicano culture, "We've always had postmodern [sic], only ours was involuntary" (Yarbro-Bejarano, "The Multiple Subject" 66). According to Gómez-Peña, the condition of straddling two cultures results in experimental art, art that acknowledges its debt to multiple reference codes. He explains, "My 'artistic space' is the intersection where the new Mexican urban poetry and the colloquial Anglo poetry meet; the intermediate stage somewhere between Mexican street theater and multimedia performance; the silence that snaps in between the *corrido* and punk . . . I am a child of crisis and cultural syncretism" (128–9).[15] Border artists exemplify what Jean-François Lyotard has belatedly called "the postmodern condition," characterized by social and economic displacement, ex-centrism, and marginalization.

While there may indeed be a theoretical convergence between the two discursive fields, the above-mentioned discussions show that this is not an unproblematic alliance. Positing an era of postmodernity can thus not lead to a unitary theory of postmodernism since such a theory would erase historical and cultural differences; instead, a writer's specific social and political position from which the questioning arises must be taken into account. Hence, readers should settle for plural manifestations of postmodernism and stress that postmodern practices can take many forms. I argue, then, for postmodern vernaculars, "languages" that are different from the standard, and that are "spoken" in such geopolitically marginal places as the Texas- or the California-Mexico borderlands. A Chicana postmodernism, then, is a regional variation of the standardized language ("high postmodernism"). To stay with the language analogy, as vernaculars such as Black English or pidgin English have had an impact on the standard language, so can Chicana postmodernism push theories of postmodernism in new directions. Specifically, these vernaculars foster a more political, multicultural version of postmodernism. In readings of the literature I point out how Chicana authors negotiate a path between "high" postmodern abstractions that gloss over political realities and humanist ideas embraced by modernity.

The definition of the term "vernacular," describing the native or indigenous language of a country or district, contains linguistic, geographic, and aesthetic components that are suggestive of the relationship between "high" postmodernism and the Chicana version. The term's root, "verna," Latin for home-born slave, may account for some of the negative connotations the word "vernacular" carries. Nonstandard languages are often related to lowly social status and are hence denigrated or recommended for improvement. Like many regional language variations, Chicana literature has been denigrated and regarded as a slave in relation to high postmodernism and mainstream literature in general. But rather than assuming a slave mentality, contemporary Chicana writers strut their vernacular.

Equally suggestive is the term's application to the arts, specifically when referring to regional art forms, those peculiar to a particular locality. In earlier uses, negative significations prevail: In 1857 G. G. Scott says, "I want to call attention to the meanness of our vernacular architecture" (*Remarks Secular and Domestic Archit.* ix; qtd. from O.E.D.). The shifting climate is evident when the Summer edition of *Daedalus* in 1977 contains the following remark: "The studies of so-called vernacular architecture (like barns) no longer seem eccentric in an atmosphere in which architecture can be defined not in terms of monuments but as any changes at all that man makes in his environment" (3; qtd. from O.E.D.). While high postmodernism certainly is "monumental" in its foregrounding of linguistic and formal experimentation, Chicana postmodernism clearly arises from the local and regional. These revaluations of "vernacular" parallel postmodernism's reassessment of the marginal and the local. The term "vernacular" applies in different forms to the literary art examined in the next few chapters. Cantú's snapshot photographs, for instance, are versions of vernacular photography and distinct from art photographs (chapter three); Cisneros's prayers in her short story "Little Miracles, Kept Promises" are vernacular versions of formal prayers (chapter four); Border Spanish in Mora's poetry is a nonstandard language towards which negative attitudes abound (chapter five). In a postcolonial move, authors such as Cisneros, Viramontes, Cantú, and Ana Castillo, provide a new valuation of their vernacular art.

An analysis of two landmark texts, Alicia Gaspar de Alba's "Literary Wetback" (1988) and Emma Pérez's *Gulf Dreams* (1996) may help to situate Chicana literature within articulations of postmodernism while simultaneously illustrating the distinctive nature of this vernacular. Particular to the vernacular of Chicana postmodernism is its creation of a dialogue between cultures, languages, and traditions (Mexican and European American), which results in new literary practices. This dialogue comes from a third space, the marginal, peripheral, noncanonized space of the borderlands, from the site of intercultural encounter.

It challenges both traditions as monolithic constructs and is defined by what D. Emily Hicks calls "multidimensional perception," or what Coco Fusco has termed "intercultural translation." In poet Pat Mora's words, "I am a child of the border . . . I know not only the pain but also the advantage of observing both sides, albeit with my own biases, of moving through two, and, in fact, multiple spaces, and selecting from both what I want to make part of me" (*Nepantla* 5–6). Theirs, to a large extent, is a postmodernism of resistance, something that Jameson did not envision in his concept of postmodernism as an all-encompassing and appropriative force. The place of enunciation, the borderlands, that third space, is precisely the space that makes resistance possible. These texts, one (Gaspar de Alba's) moderately, the other (Pérez's) radically experimental, set in motion a dynamic whereby the textual feature of hybridization and syncretism are clearly linked to the socio-historical context in which they were produced. In other words, it is through their self-reflexive dialogue with European American and Mexican traditions that these texts can be termed postmodern. Both share an epistemological questioning that is characteristic of the postmodern era. Both also, unlike dominant discussions of postmodernism, prominently focus on categories of race/ethnicity and gender.

In 1988, one year after the publication of Gloria Anzaldúa's *Borderlands/La Frontera: The New Mestiza,* Chicana poet Gaspar de Alba published a piece, entitled "Literary Wetback," in the *Massachusetts Review.* "Literary Wetback," like *Borderlands*, is a generic hybrid, blending prose and poetry in its exploration of the writer's border consciousness—her process of becoming Chicana.[16] "Literary Wetback" narrates the writer's beginnings, and tells of how she finds her location on the border between Mexico and the United States. She begins her piece with the words, "When Bostonians hear me speak Spanish and ask me what country I'm from, I say I come from the border between Tejas and Méjico" (288). Gaspar de Alba emphatically (re-)claims the geographic site of the border, that precarious and marginal space betwixt and between nations, languages, cultures, and traditions, as her country. She continues, "Nobody asks what side of the border I'm talking about, and I don't tell them, mainly because, to me, the border is the border, and it would not make any sense to divide it into sides" (288). This statement suggests the border as a third term, the site between stable poles where national, linguistic, and cultural divisions don't hold. Gaspar de Alba thus creates a location and new subject positions for the border person.

While the border refers to a specific geographic site, it also becomes the dominant trope of the piece. The poem "La Frontera," which concludes Gaspar de Alba's reflections, personifies the border as a woman, a "sleeping beauty," whose geography follows that of the female body and who beckons the speaker and invites her into her arms. While the first stanza celebrates the border's seductive nature, the last two lines shock readers with their blunt references to immigration: "both/sides leaking sangre/y sueños" (292). The alliterative linking of "sangre y sueños" (blood and dreams) refers to the concrete social and historical problematic of the U.S./Mexico border, the Central and South American immigrants' hopes for better lives, and the dangers to their lives during the crossing, as the deaths of fifteen in the Arizona desert in June 2001 remind us. The speaker then approaches, "mystified by the sleek Río Grande" and "the silent lloronas, "references to the Mexican American cultural icon of the weeping woman who drowned her children in the river after being abandoned by her husband. At the end the speaker proclaims, "Yo también me he acostado con ella,/crossed that cold bed, wading/toward a hunched coyote" (292). This is an important moment in the poem as it provides a vision of the writer as activist: the speaker/poet places herself within the context of a community of immigrants/ migrants, one who has followed the migrations of her people. Like other Chicana writers, Gaspar de Alba engages in an exchange with cultural traditions (la llorona), creates and modifies those traditions, and records her culture.

In the above poem, the border already appears in various guises, as geopolitical artifact, seductive woman (both life-sustaining and cause of death) and myth-inspiring waters. The poet further uses the trope of the border metaphorically to portray the speaker's subject position. In this location, she finds herself moving between worlds and between two languages, English and Spanish: "At home I was Mexican and spoke only Spanish, and yet we celebrated Thanksgiving and the Fourth of July. At school, my language was English and we pledged allegiance to the American flag, and yet we prayed to the Virgen de Guadalupe" (290). This linguistic flexibility, an expression of, in María Lugones's words, "world travelling" ("Playfulness") is seen as enriching for the bicultural individual. Gaspar de Alba comments: "Chicanos are lucky because our heritage straddles two countries and feeds off two traditions" (291). However, this retrospective insight is preceded by painful awareness and recurring concerns with identity, and specifically, with the cultural schizophrenia that results from the constant movement between stable and fixed locations. The speaker had to learn to live with this double consciousness and writes, "cultural schizophrenia set in early. At home I was pura

Mejicana. At school I was an American citizen" (289).[17] Thematically, then, Gaspar de Alba depicts the process of constantly crossing borders and its effects on the subject; formally, she illustrates this process through extensive code-switching.

Gaspar de Alba's piece further traverses gender boundaries as it explodes traditional images of Mexican American women. In "Domingo Means Scrubbing," the adolescent speaker's irreverence and performance of gender is demonstrated when she lists her small rebellions against the family's Sunday rituals: she hides the quarter meant for beggars under her tongue "like a host," sneaks a beer when the tías exchange Pepito jokes in the kitchen, and plays Dad because she's the oldest cousin. Juxtaposed with this spunkiness are social strictures aimed at proper gender socialization and ultimate resigned reaffirmation of borders, as at the end of the poem when "'Amá com[es] out of the house/to drag the girls inside/pa' lavar los dishes" (291).

The example of Gaspar de Alba's text shows that Chicana literature and discourses of postmodernism intersect, overlap, and criss-cross each other's terrain. The experimental nature of the text, specifically its dissolution of generic boundaries and its linguistic experimentation in form of code-switching, align it with the textual experimentation that is the hallmark of postmodernism. Like poststructuralists and theorists of the postmodern, Gaspar de Alba uses the border trope, suggesting the dissolution of borders and boundaries during postmodernity. Gaspar de Alba, like Anzaldúa, Sandoval, and Pérez, theorizes and revalidates marginal locations while implicitly or explicitly aligning those locations with postmodernism.[18] Further, Gaspar de Alba's portrayal of Third World women's identity as fluid and shifting, not only recalls Sandoval's "differential consciousness", but also Gilles Deleuze and Félix Guattari's theoretizations of schizophrenia.

Throughout the text, Gaspar de Alba deals with social, ethnic, and gender issues that commonly don't find representation in many theories of high postmodernism. Moreover, Gaspar de Alba employs border tropes with historical specificity unknown to high postmodernism. Despite the generic hybridization and textual experimentation, Gaspar de Alba's, and, I would argue, that of many Chicana writers, is a postmodernism that is less visible in formal play than in a fundamental challenging of systems of thought and cultural assumptions. My contention here and throughout this study is that there are significant areas where the literature and theory overlap, but that Chicana literature forges new directions for postmodernism.

This is not to say that Chicana writers do not engage in what I would call "high postmodern" play with form. Emma Pérez's novel *Gulf Dreams* (1996), for instance, deserves to be mentioned along with other "high" postmodern authors such as Kathy Acker, John Barth, or Thomas Pynchon. *Gulf Dreams* is a postmodern *Künstlerroman* in its disjointed, non-linear narration and episodic structure that not only mirrors the nameless first-person narrator's fragmented identity but also the process of reconstructing a painful past through memory. The text's self-referentiality and narcissism further reflects the narrator's self-absorption. Her attempts to break out from cycles of abuse take center stage in the novel, and the narrative is propelled by both her unfulfilled desire for her unnamed female friend and the sexual abuse she experienced during infancy, childhood, and adolescence. The story then amplifies incidents that suggest her life at the intersection of her gender (i.e., sexual abuse), sexuality (her lesbianism), race (institutionalized racism that emerges from educational, medical, and judicial authorities), and class (poverty and children working along with parents in the cotton fields). Despite the novel's traditional three-part structure (Confession—Trial—Desire), metanarrative comments such as, "I don't believe in endings. I believe in the imagination, its pleasure indelible, transgressive, a dream" (157), suggest its inconclusive nature and lack of teleological development.

As the novel's non-linear structure disrupts conventions of reading, the short vignettes also challenge conventional social practices and behavioral norms such as scripts for social interaction, which the narrator calls "blueprints." Such blueprints, she comments, "that scientifically sketched out life's reason disillusioned me" (51). Thus Pérez's strategies lead us to question the ideologies of heterosexual romance through the narrator's unnamed male-identified friend, whose "husband owned her, sapping her, wanting every piece of her" (46) as well as acceptable social scripts for Mexican American women. When the narrator first visits the friend's family, she observes:

> No one knew why I had come. To see my new friend, they thought. To link families with four sisters who would be friends longer than their lifetimes through children who would bond them at baptismal rites. Comadres. We would become intimate friends sharing coffee, gossip, and heartaches. We would endure the female life-cycle—adolescence, marriage, menopause, death, and even divorce, before or after menopause, before or after death. (13)

The very next section, however, begins with the terse statement of her "forbidden" desire that shows how her expectations clash with those of her environment: "I had not come for that. I had come for her kiss" (13).

But *Gulf Dreams* does not stop with a challenge to heterosexuality; it shocks with its violence and iconoclastic depiction of a pathological lesbian character who does not fit neatly into prefabricated categories. Nor does it create a neat binary of abuser vs. abused, victim vs. victimizer; instead, it complicates matters by creating the life of Chencho, Ermilia's rapist, who forms the focus of the second section of the novel, to the extent that the reader gains insight into his life of abuse as well. By foregrounding that "the Anglo media pictured [Mexican men] like greasy boys with slicked back hair, baggy chino slacks and plaid untucked shirts" (116), the readers' indictment of the men portrayed in the novel is put on hold; instead, morally/ethically speaking, readers find themselves on constantly shifting ground.

A third of the way into the book, the narrator's comment, "Excavating, digging deeper, like an archaeologist uncovering remnants, piecing together what she has only imagined for years" (50), assumes various important meanings. On the one hand, it refers to the narrator's prolonged process of facing her painful past, but on the other hand, it can be seen as a metaphor of storytelling and metanarrative comment on the processes of narration. It can also be read as a reference to Foucauldian archaeology, his insistence on uncovering traces of the unheard, the invisible. In this signification, much of Chicana literature is such an archaeology that gives voice to the voiceless, most importantly, in Pérez's book, the Chicana lesbian. In her book *The Decolonial Imaginary: Writing Chicanas into History*, Pérez refers to Foucault's archaeology as challenging "disciplines, their categories, their grids and cells be exploded, opened up, confronted, inverted, and subverted" (xvi) and "focuses on the transformation of discursive fields" (11). Certainly this novel, as do other postmodern works, transforms the discursive field of "novel" and of the category "Chicana novel." It also suggests the usefulness of looking at Chicana literature through the lens of postmodernism.[19]

Such an explosion and opening up of the disciplines has been facilitated by postmodernism itself. Postmodernism has led to a "crisis of representation" affecting many disciplines, and this study benefits from such methodological scrutiny, ways in which humanities disciplines have redefined themselves. Most illuminating are recent developments in the fields of geography, history, ethnography, photography, and linguistics. Postmodernism has also drawn attention to the ways in which we largely operate from within existing academic barriers and has prepared the ground for a thorough investigation of interdisciplinary connections. While postmodern/poststructuralist theory and Chicana texts are certainly in the foreground of this project, my discussions of the primary texts are informed by recent feminist and postcolonial theory, as well as cultural, transnational, and global studies.

While much Chicana writing shares with postmodern theory a rejection of monolithic, unilateral constructions, an examination of intersections between the two brings to postmodernism a critical examination of the theory's Euro-centric bias. Postmodernism in itself, in these articulations, has become monological, a new master theory.[20] An engagement with feminist and multicultural critics has rendered it commonplace by now to question the origins of postmodernism. Many have argued that multicultural literatures precede postmodernism. For instance, Stephanie Athey, focusing on African American literature, has observed that "the fragmentation experienced and recorded by those in socially and politically disenfranchised groups has both prefigured and propelled the more generalized ... 'decentering' of postmodern subjects" (170).[21] Similarly, Sandoval asserts that differential consciousness, once a necessity for socially marginalized citizens, is now made available by a postmodern cultural dynamic to all first world subjects (22). Another way in which this vernacular confronts high postmodern theory is in its specification of historical context. All too often postmodern theories gloss over political realities and do not ask what is at stake when boundaries are blurred, genres are transgressed, and signifiers are played with. Chicana postmodernists write against abstraction, confront these questions head-on, and pose challenges to such postmodern celebrations.

This study examines specific intersections among Chicana and postmodern/poststructuralist discourses in the form of a series of "conversations." Each of the subsequent chapters therefore explores an issue central to both postmodern theory and Chicana literature: the trope of borders and boundaries (chapter one), space and subjectivity (chapter two), literary realism (chapter three), genre (chapter four), and language (chapter five). An analysis of the literary texts illustrates Pérez's contention that Chicana theory can be found in unexpected places, in prefaces to anthologies as well as in the literature itself (*Decolonial Imaginary*). Included in the study are readings of autobiographies, poetry, short stories, and novels by nationally acclaimed Chicana authors: Gloria Anzaldúa, Sandra Cisneros, Ana Castillo, Norma Elía Cantú, Pat Mora, and Helena María Viramontes. Readers will find that Anzaldúa's work occupies a prominent position in this study because of the great explanatory value of her theories for the Chicana writing I examine. Her

writing, along with that of Jacques Derrida, will serve as a road map. Readings of
literary texts are supplemented by references to cultural and historical debates
around migration and immigration, language practices and attitudes, and
representation, which surface through a variety of textual artifacts, including
popular cultural narratives, newspaper narratives, *telenovelas* (Mexican American
soap operas), photographs, and oral stories that inform of U.S. American and
Mexican cultural values. These authors' works represent a range of stylistic
experimentation; all are postmodern in their challenges to traditional constructs of
space, realism, genre, borders, and language. At the same time, all engage critically
with these contemporary theories and modify them. In this way, Chicana writers
dance around and between the poles of humanism and postmodernism.

Chapters one and two form a unit in that both focus on spatial tropes in
literature and in theory. The first contrasts rhetorical constructions of the border
in poststructuralist discourses with official constructions of the international
boundary line between the U.S. and Mexico as revealed in newspaper narratives
published between 1998–2001, and figurations of the border in Gloria Anzaldúa's
Borderlands/La Frontera: The New Mestiza. I suggest that Anzaldúa's poetic depiction
of the border and her focus on immigration and labor relations serve as important
correctives to a postmodern rhetoric that celebrates borders as rather permeable
and fluid phenomena as well as to nationalist sentiments that suggest barring
access. Chapter two focuses on spatial tropes as representations of subjectivity.
Poststructuralist discourses have usefully dislodged notions of stable centers,
places, and identities, but pay scarce attention to the concrete power relations
inscribed in certain geographic locations. In contrast, I propose a more historically
specific reading that enables us to see first, how Anzaldúa's borderlands sometimes
painfully forge mestiza identity; second, how Pat Mora's poetry presents liminal
spaces as metaphors of social locations and concrete class conflicts among
Chicanas; and third, how Helena María Viramontes's *Under the Feet of Jesus* critiques
postmodern tropes of nomadism and migrancy by pointing out the material and
economic limits of mobility.

Chapters three and four shift from rhetorical tropes to issues of representation
through discussions of the literary mode of realism and the category of genre. The
third chapter focuses on how Norma Elía Cantú's autobiographical work *Canícula:
Snapshots of a Girlhood en la frontera* negotiates both poststructuralist theories of the
impossibility of accurately reflecting reality and traditional realist representation
through its frequently ironic inclusion of snapshot photographs. In this chapter I

argue that Cantú, despite her obvious awareness of its pitfalls, employs realist techniques strategically and for didactic purposes by evoking the discourses of autobiography, ethnography, historiography, and photography for the supposed "certainty" they afford. Chapter four shows that the works of Ana Castillo *(So Far From God)* and Sandra Cisneros ("Little Miracles, Kept Promises") incorporate and deconstruct narratives that derive from diverse cultures: the European American family saga and the Mexican *telenovela*, the short story, and Mexican American oral traditions. Through their generic hybridization, these authors, like many postmodern writers, defy notions of "generic purity," what Jacques Derrida has called the "Law of Genre," but firmly root their literary transgressions in bicultural experiences.

The final chapter focuses on linguistic *mestizaje* in Pat Mora's poetry, works that innovatively use code-switching between English and Spanish. I argue that they simultaneously express the postmodern condition and refine current theories of postmodernism. While postmodern theories stress linguistic play, or, in Derrida's terms, "the play of signifier," they treat language as an autonomous system, disconnected from social and historical forces. In contrast, I suggest that interlingualism in Mora's work can best be understood when seen in the context of language debates and language attitudes in the southwestern United States.

Chapter 1

Narratives of the Border: Postmodern Hybridity, Barbed Wire Fences, and *Mestizaje*

My fingers wanted to reach through the wire fence, not to touch it, not to feel it, but to break it down, to melt it down with what I did not understand. The burning was not there to be understood. Something was burning, the side of me that knew I was treated different, would always be treated different because I was born on a particular side of a fence, a fence that separated me from others, that separated me from a past, that separated me from a country I did not love because it demanded something of me I could not give. Something was burning now, and if I could have grasped the source of that rage and held it in my fist, I would have melted that fence. Someone built that fence; someone could tear it down. Maybe I could tear it down; maybe I was the one; maybe then I would no longer be separated.

Benjamin Alire Sáenz (207)

No border is guaranteed, inside or out. Try it.

Jacques Derrida, "Living On" (78)

What critics of the INS ignore is the inconvenient fact that a nation that cannot control its own borders is putting its very nationhood in hazard.

("On the Border")

In her 1994 essay, "Spatial Metaphor and the Politics of Empowerment: Mapping a Place for Feminism and Postmodernism in Geography," Patricia Price-Chalita writes, "knowledge, and the power that is bound up with that knowledge is often constructed in spatial terms. Thus it comes as no surprise that feminists might choose the spatial as the site for contesting such relations of power" (237).[1] One such spatial metaphor or trope is the border, the *site* where a variety of contemporary discourses intersect. As Jacques Derrida's epigraph to this chapter indicates, postmodern and poststructuralist discourses, for instance, celebrate a variety of border crossings and, critics suggest, rather abstractly construct borders as permeable phenomena. Derrida's strangely absolutist statement, "*No* border is guaranteed" and his provocative invitation to "try it," implies the risk-free nature of such an enterprise. Chicana writing, like that of the feminist geographers Price-Chalita refers to, tends to construct borders as more contested sites. As we have seen in the previous chapter, Alicia Gaspar de Alba's "Literary Wetback" employs the border trope metaphorically to create a new location for the bicultural speaking subject while not losing sight of border's meanings as geopolitical artifact. Her text is symptomatic of the border as recurring motif in Chicano/a discourses.[2] By focusing on Gloria Anzaldúa's *Borderlands/La Frontera: The New Mestiza* (1987), I argue that while Anzaldúa's experimental text depicts formal similarities with postmodern and poststructural border discourses, the work also provides an important corrective to the postmodern celebratory rhetoric. Through an examination of formal and thematic border crossings in *Borderlands/La Frontera*, I suggest that this work points out how postmodern theories gloss over political realities. To do so, this chapter is divided into three parts: first, I will focus on rhetorical constructions of borders in Derridean poststructuralist discourse, a discourse that affected postmodern theorizing; second, on official constructions of the international boundary line between the U.S. and Mexico as revealed in the rhetoric of newspaper narratives; and third, on figurations of the border in Anzaldúa's text.

In his effort to question a multiplicity of borders, Jacques Derrida's work heavily relies on spatial metaphors of borders, edges, frames, limits, and demarcations. Two works in particular, "Living On: BORDER LINES" and *Glas,* dramatize his concern with boundaries, here the boundaries of a text, by drawing attention to the spatial dimensions of the page. The former text consists of two simultaneous essays, both on Shelley's *The Triumph of Life* and on Blanchot's *L'arrêt de mort*, demarcated by a horizontal dividing line whereby the essay in the lower portion of the page ("BORDER LINES") appears as though it were a footnote to that in the upper portion ("Living On"). Speaking of the text in the lower part of the page, Derrida helpfully suggests, "Let them read this band as a telegram or a film for developing" ("BORDER LINES" 77). *Glas* draws attention to the role of the theory book as a material object first of all through its unusual format; in contrast to most critical books published by university presses it has the large size and layout of an art book. The pages contain two columns of prose, each with varying type and font sizes, and each occasionally broken up by short interpolations that are let into the text. The one column consists of a discussion of Hegel, the other one of the *enfant terrible* of French literature, Jean Genet. In addition to the text(s), *Glas* invites reflection on the visual discourse it offers.

Both pieces disrupt traditional reading practices—do we read "Living On" first and then return to page one and read "BORDER LINES," or do we read the text page by page?— and effectively *perform* their theoretical challenges to the notion of text as a self-enclosed unit through constant cross-references and resonances from one text to the other. These essays set themselves up as textual explications of Shelley and Blanchot, but evaluation and interpretation soon become the "pretexts" ("Living On" 77) that allow Derrida to concern himself instead self-reflexively with issues of textuality and translation. In "Living On: BORDER LINES" he asks "What are the borderlines of a text?" ("Living On" 85) and in the lower band states, "I wish to pose the question of the *bord*, the edge, the border, and the *bord de mer*, the shore . . ." ("BORDER LINES" 82), clarifying in the upper band, ". . . all those boundaries that form the running border of what used to be called a text" ("Living On" 83). He continues by arguing, "What has happened . . . *is a sort of overrun [débordement]* that spoils all these boundaries and divisions and forces us to extend the accredited concept, the dominant notion of a text" ("Living On" 83–4; emphasis added). From the beginning of the piece, where he muses on the implications of the title "Living On" and establishes it as a quotation and furthermore as polysemic, Derrida demonstrates that the boundary, "the upper edge" of his text, is multilayered and points outside of itself. The text loses its footing, loses sight of the line of demarcation between text and not-text, submerging its shore. According to Derrida, this overrun produces endless efforts to resist it and to rebuild old partitions. A text then is not autonomous, "some content enclosed in a book or its margins, but a differential network, a fabric of traces referring endlessly to something other than itself, to other differential traces" ("Living On" 84).[3]

"Gnawing away at the border" (Derrida, *Margins* xxiii)—manifested elsewhere in Derrida's attack on classical literary theory's notions of generic purity and his advocacy of generic boundary crossings[4]—has become a hallmark of poststructuralist and postmodern discussions of literature. These discourses stress the fluidity and permeability of borders, and replace the norm of purity with one of hybridization and syncretism. Its rhetoric celebrates crossing borders and blurring boundaries while liminality and interstitial existence become characteristics of the postmodern condition. The proliferation in the last decade of criticism that seeks to deconstruct boundaries testifies to the empowering nature of this

Figure 1: Border crossing at Sasabe, Sonora. AP Photo: Guillermo Arias

approach: borders exist to be transgressed, and that transgression affords seemingly endless ludic possibilities.[5] For the purposes of this chapter, I would like to point out that in this rhetoric, borders are used as metaphors that denote any dividing line between two stable entities configured as bipolar opposites. Border rhetoric functions as part of the poststructuralist project of deconstruction; it is part of the effort to destabilize metaphysics and a reaction against structuralism, its notion of centers, and its hermeneutics of binary oppositions. For poststructuralism, the ultimate goal is to undermine these oppositions.

While poststructuralist theory generally elides reference to geographic borders, in the geopolitical sphere, borders separating one country from another historically have been crucial in constructing a sense of nationhood and identity. Since the treaty of Rome in 1957, however, this sense of nation-states guaranteed by borders has been crumbling in many parts of Europe, a tendency that was intensified with the collapse of the Berlin wall and the end of the cold war.[6] Symptomatic of post-national thinking on this continent is the North American Free Trade Agreement (NAFTA; signed in 1992), but despite a new era of opening borders, economic globalization, and transnational capitalism, the United States is currently going through another period of strengthening its southern border with Mexico.

Figure 2: Texas-Mexcio Boder at Brownsville. Photograph by Lara Hooper

Ironically we are witnessing the simultaneous deployment of rhetoric deriving from a post-national or postmodern economic environment and a recurrence, or rather persistence, of national*ist* discourses. Symptomatic of such contradictions is a *New York Times* report on a photography exhibition of life on the border between El Paso and Ciudad Juárez. Commentator Charles Bowden explains that "Juarez is an exhibit of the fabled New World Order in which capital moves easily and labor is trapped by borders" (Goldberg 44).[7]

Indicative of this contradiction also is a recent *New York Times* article celebrating the new border fence in Nogales, Arizona, as "a grand piece of architecture" (Verhovek "Mexican Border" A17). The wall is intended to be "forbidding yet friendly, inimical but somehow inviting all at the same time" (A1). Officials insist that this architectural feat, bearing a striking resemblance to the Berlin wall and replacing an ugly, rusting fence built from steel military landing mats, is not a wall but a "fence." The architectural design—large blue-trimmed Plexiglass windows, a salmon color "inlaid with multicolored stone chips and with tiles that eventually may be decorated with children's art" (A17)—suggest the light, permeability, and openness of a kinder, gentler border. Its purpose is to "evoke the friendship between the two nations" and, according to architect Peter A. Dubin, to "[open] up the borders between North and South" (Verhovek A1; A17).

Figure 3: U.S.-Mexico Border at Nuevo Progresso.
Photograph by Joseph Jozwiak

Officials tend to employ a kinship rhetoric when discussing U.S. and Mexican "sister" cities separated by the wall—all part of the same human family.[8] Before September 11, 2001, such notions of the border as symbol of unity were espoused at the highest level of U.S. foreign policy. At a joint conference with Mexican foreign minister Jorge Cateñeda, Secretary of State Colin Powell said, "Our common border is no longer a line that divides us, but a region that unites our nations, reflecting our common aspirations, values, and culture" (Weiner A13).

However, aesthetics and semantic manipulation cannot obscure the fact that this fence operates to solidify very un-postmodern notions of a unified nation-state that creates a U.S.-American insider and a Mexican "Other". In the same article, officials are cited to claim that the wall must be an effective barrier, "resistant to repeated physical assault by means such as welding torches, chisels, hammers, firearms, climbing over or penetration by vehicles" (Verhovek A1). Walls, and not fences, are on the minds of the lawmakers as well. The consistent efforts of the Republican Congress in the 1990s to strengthen border surveillance, with repeated calls by Patrick Buchanan and Newt Gingrich for an extension of the fence along the entire border (Schodolski 28), go hand in hand with a resurgence of nationalist rhetoric. In 1996 Debbie Nathan reported that during the Clinton administration, while other government agencies were being trimmed, the Border Patrol's budget swelled to $585 million, up 80% since 1992, with an increase of 27% in the number of agents (13). In general, the motto is "we're taking back our border," and discussions focus on *sealing* "the nation's borders" through a "wall of agents" (Cavazos A19), by "building higher and higher walls" (Baro A16), or through well-funded operations with suggestive names like "Operation Gatekeeper," "Operation Gulf Shield," or "Operation Blockade," later renamed "Operation Hold the Line." As one commentator sympathetic to renewed financial and hardware infusions to the border patrol writes, "what critics of the INS ignore is the inconvenient fact that a nation that cannot control its own borders is putting its very nationhood in hazard" ("On the Border").

The idea that Washington "reassert" control over the border ("Run from the Border") also hints at the top-down legislation that oftentimes ignores local culture. As at least one writer points out when discussing one recent border operation in Brownsville, Texas, "Operation Rio Grande," the project responds not to an outcry from the community but to national sentiments. In contrast to their counterparts in El Paso or San Diego, for instance, Rio Grande Valley residents enjoy "amicable relations with their Mexican neighbor." Both business and political leaders pride themselves on close ties with their Mexican counterparts (Cavazos A19). These disruptions intensified after September 11, 2001, when tough enforcement of immigration laws led Border Patrol agents to put an end to unofficial rowboat crossings in the Big Bend area in Texas, an area where the river is not a dividing line but where marriages and families extend on both sides of the Rio Grande (Yardley A1).

As barbed wire is put up, "fences" are built, and border guards receive military backing, the rhetoric of family and friendship is more than challenged and replaced by one that views the border as a war-zone. Lamar Smith, Democrat from San Antonio and chair of the House subcommittee on immigration, observed, "drug-smuggling, alien-smuggling, and their attendant violence and corruption are increasing all along the border, and I am deeply concerned about our ability to *combat* this wave of criminal activity in an effective manner" (Jackson A9; emphasis added). Military rhetoric pervades the media narratives of the border. The border is constructed as "huge" and "untamed," a "darkness of vice and smuggling," and must guard against "hordes of illegals" that "pour over the border" like a tidal wave. These stories stress the need to "fight back," to form "lines of attack." Immigrants, and by implication Mexicans, are constructed as the enemy. Critics, on the other hand, warn of establishing an armed corridor and frequently compare the situation at the border with East Berlin.

This military rhetoric, fueled by sensationalistic portrayals of undocumented immigration, is strongly backed by federal actions.[9] Since 1989 the border area has witnessed increased deployment of military units for training and patrols, and of hardware, including infra-red sensors, military satellites, and reconnaissance planes (O'Connell "Sky" A1). The joint efforts of law-enforcement agencies (Border Patrol) and the military with, as commentators suggest, fundamentally incompatible cultures and missions—on the one hand to preserve order, and on the other hand to "find, close with, and destroy the enemy" ("Run from the Border")[10]—led to disastrous effects in the summer of 1997 when a teenager was killed by a U.S. Marine during a border surveillance project—the first killing of an American civilian by military gunfire since Kent State in 1970. Military patrols were called off shortly after this fatal incident, though the military provides continued support in "document analysis, translation, aerial reconnaissance, engineering, training, and secured transportation of drug evidence" (O'Connell and Hoffman A10). In May of 1998 the House voted again to enlist the military to help patrol borders in the war against drug smuggling and illegal immigration, which, however, met with considerable reserve from the Pentagon. Texas Democrat Chet Edwards warned, "this would make the Texas-Mexico border look like East Berlin after World War II" (Raum A15).[11] Nonetheless, since 2001, army and marines have again increased their presence to stop possible terrorists from crossing the border ("Militarization").

While the shooting of the teenager may have been an isolated incident, violence and deaths are nonetheless pervasive in this war zone. Newspaper narratives annually focus on deaths related to border crossings, in the Kenedy county desert in South Texas, once called *El Desierto de los Muertes*, or in the desert territory of Arizona. Critics of border patrol operations had predicted that strengthening patrols in the highly populated areas of the Rio Grande Valley, El Paso, and San Diego in 1995 would increases risks of death because undocumented immigrants are squeezed to more desolate areas and more hostile terrain (Nathan 13). A 2001 study by the Center for Immigration Research at the University of Houston, *Causes and Trends in Migrant Deaths along the Mexican Border,*

1985–1998, confirms such fears. The report found that deaths from weather-related causes have risen dramatically since 1995. By 1998 they were three times more common than when undocumented immigration crested in the mid 1980s (Eschbach et al). The Border Patrol responded to this humanitarian crisis with "Operation Lifesaver," with guards donning life-saving equipment. From 1993–1997 alone, at least 1,185 people had drowned, died of exposure or dehydration, or been hit by automobiles while trying to cross the border (Verhovek, "Silent" A1+). Dangers also await migrants from rivaling smuggling rings and bandits, as when seventeen were found dead in a truck near Victoria, Texas, in May of 2003. More recently, a number of armed paramilitary groups and vigilante patrols have emerged with pseudo-military titles such as "Civil Homeland Defense" and "Operation Falcon" who, in the name of national security, guard ranches against illegal immigrants.

As we have seen, Derrida views borders as metaphorical constructs and crossing borders as a compositional practice. Boundaries, deeply entrenched in Western epistemology, are remnants of Enlightenment philosophy and must be overrun. In Derridean border narratives, crossings are uninvolved in power relations and hence relatively risk-free. In contrast, the narrative that emerges from newpaper reports, while at times mystifying U.S.-Mexico relations as friendly, upholds the necessity of borders in the national interest. In Chicano/a discourse, the border has long been an important concept, and Gloria Anzaldúa's *Borderlands/La Frontera* is a key text in studies of the borderlands, one that comments on and participates in those historical and political discourses around the U.S.-Mexico border.[12] As Hector Calderón points out, Anzaldúa employs a "historical and metaphoric vision of the border in order to bring down barriers and build political bridges" ("Texas Border" 23). Anzaldúa's book negotiates a path between Derridean and media narratives. Her desire to bring down barriers and transgress boundaries resembles Derrida's deconstruction to a certain extent, but she goes beyond abstraction by positioning herself clearly at the specific geographical site of crossing, the U.S.-Mexican border. Her work further presents an important shift in perspective from that of official narratives, as it gives voice to the Mexican and Mexican American Other.

Like Derrida's "Living On: BORDERLINES," the book is divided into two parts that echo and play off each other: the first is entitled "*Atravesando Fronteras*/Crossing Borders" and consists of seven autobiographical essays, complete with footnotes and scholarly apparatus, but interspersed with occasional poems; the second, entitled "*Agitado Viento*/Ehécatl, the Wind" consists of six chapters of poetry. Like Derrida's piece, the book stages a challenge to the unity and autonomy of each part through its multiple cross-references. Conceived originally as a collection of poetry with a ten-page introduction, the first part of the book grew into a 100-page long treatise (Kate Adams 134). Similar to Derrida's challenge to the production and consumption of the "theory book," Anzaldúa foregrounds the process of reading through the marketing of the book itself. Kate Adams comments on how the reading of individual poems is to a large extent determined by the poems' "containers:" usually sold in small volumes of works by a single poet, or in anthologies, poetry may become a "formulaic," and the reading of poetry an experience that is devoid of context. Instead, Anzaldúa embeds her poems in "an informative net of materials surrounding or accompanying them" (132). This strategy, Adams concludes, "denies poetry as a discrete genre the purity or exclusivity that the slim volume, the anthology, and a great deal of academic discourse help to provide it" (132). Part one thus does not coincide with the poetry but nourishes it by furnishing Derridean traces; it functions as commentary, context, and amplification, and clearly encourages crisscrossing textual borders.[13]

Borderlands further displays postmodern formal characteristics, including montage, pastiche, briccolage, and, perhaps most overtly, generic hybridization. As a biomythography, the work blends prose and poetry, autobiography and essay, historiography, fiction, and myth. Characteristically, Anzaldúa comments that she delights in "jump[ing] over the fence into another genre" (Perry 24).[14] On a thematic level, the work is known for its development of Anzaldúa's vision of the "new mestiza," the ultimate border crosser and locus of cultural exchange, whose consciousness is characterized by hybridity, mutability, and malleability. Much has been written about the new mestiza and the vision she embodies, as also about Anzaldúa's mythic invocation of the goddess Coatlicue, who signifies a rupture in the everyday world (Anzaldúa 46), and who functions in the text as a symbol of fusing opposites and transcending dualistic thinking.[15]

A focus on some of her much-neglected narrative poetry—full of images of borders, edges, and margins—reveals how individual poems *perform* the liberatory potential of border crossing outlined in the first part of the book. The third poetry section is entitled, "Crossers *y otros atravesados*," and parallels part four of the prose chapters, entitled "*La herencia de Coatlicue*/The Coatlicue State," the most fragmented and poetic of the prose sections, and in Jane Hedley's words "the narrative fulcrum" of the text (44) where Anzaldúa enacts the crossing the poet has prepared for in the previous chapters. As the chapter explains, to become a visionary, the poet/prophet descends into the underworld and reemerges after she has been entered by the goddess, equipped with knowledge of mental processes different from rational ones and ready now to assume her role as poetic shaman.

Two poems in particular, "Poets Have Strange Eating Habits" and "Interface," enact the spiritual possibilities of border crossings. The first poem of the section, "Poets" (*Borderlands* 140–41), dramatizes the speaker's transformations as she attempts to achieve the Coatlicue state. Anzaldúa tells the truth "slant," in Emily Dickinson's terms, by representing this spritual transformation through a lyrical evocation of the poet and her mare's flight off a cliff. This flight symbolizes the poet's plunge into the cave of the imagination, a plunge that is fraught with anticipation but also with fear. As Anzaldúa writes in part one, there is a "resistance to knowing, to letting go . . . to opening myself to the alien other where I am out of control, not on patrol. The outcome on the other side unknown, the reins falling and the horses plunging blindly over the crumbling path rimming the edge of the cliff, plunging into its thousand foot drop" (48). In the poem, the move is compared to an Aztec sacrifice, and the speaker displaces her own hesitation onto her horse: she has to "coax and whip the balking mare / to the edge" until she dives "off the high cliff."

Crossing over into alien territory is familiar to undocumented border crossers who might see themselves at the edge of a cliff, hesitant for fear of transgression. The vertical motion of plunging into an abyss is linked by analogy to the horizontal motion of border crossing—a simultaneous move downward and across. As Anzaldúa explains earlier, "It is her reluctance to cross over, to make a hole in the fence and walk across, to cross the river, to take that flying leap into the dark, that drives her to escape" (49). Immigration—crossing over—becomes "taking a flying leap in the dark" (49). However, once taken, the plunge enables the poet to "peer over the edge," and leads to repeatedly "coax[ing] and whip[ping] the balking mare" to "take that plunge again," until "jumping off cliffs" becomes an addiction (141). The habitual border crosser, undocumented alien and poet alike, is privileged in his/her familiarity with other modes of consciousness.

In contrast to the spiritual experience the poem portrays, the very worldly and ironic title sets up images of ingestion. What the poet eats is the world, much like Coatlicue and earth who "open[s] and swallow[s] us, plunging us into the underworld where the soul resides" (46). The poem is framed by this image of transgressing the borders of the body: the mare's "body caves into itself / through the hole / my mouth" and at the end "Taking deep breaths eyes closed / *me la tragó todita.*" To demonstrate the poet's ability to fuse opposites, Anzaldúa weaves in images of borders and binary oppositions of material/spiritual, inward/outward, dusk/dawn, sky/earth. The poetic "I" is simultaneously "eagle fetus" and "live serpent", associated in Nahuatl symbology with sky (masculine) and earth (feminine); like an eagle, she has "feathers growing out of my skin," and like a serpent she is "tunneling here tunneling there" into the underworld, a motif set up in "Protean Being." This *both/and* rather than *either/or* position is crucial to Anzaldúa's inclusive and transgressive vision. The state of embracing contradiction is the state of the border person.

The final poem of this section also explores the idea of transgression and transformation. The title, "Interface" (*Borderlands* 148–52), refers to a space in between, a metaphorical borderland and "home" of the mestiza independent of the speaker's physical location. It is the space where the two stable poles of a binary system, defined here as "material vs. spiritual," interact. In this narrative poem, the speaker looks :

> at the edges of things
> my eyes going wide watering,
>   objects blurring
> Where before there'd only been empty space
>   I sensed layers and layers (148)

This heightened consciousness expands the speaker's field of vision so that she opens herself to the presence of an "alien" other and has a lesbian encounter with her. "Alien," of course, is a term with rich resonances in a book about borders, a term that Anzaldúa expropriates from the mythology of the border ("Gloria Anzaldúa's" Yarbro-Bejarano 23), as well as a term that grounds the poetry through alluding to its specific meanings in U.S.-American discourses. Opening oneself up to the alien presence is uncomfortable—as the speaker states, "I am again an alien in new territory" (48)—but it is also spiritually liberating. She comments,

> At first it was hard to stay
>   on the border between
> the physical world

and hers.
It was only there at the interface
      that we could see each other. (148)

Anzaldúa continues to explore the duality of material and spiritual, mind and body through juxtaposing the speaker's physical existence with the friend's immateriality:

      We lay enclosed by margins, hems,
where only we existed.
      She was stroking stroking my arms
my legs, marveling at their solidity,
      the warmth of my flesh, its smell.
Then I touched her.
      Fog, she felt like dense fog,
the color of smoke. (150)

To anchor this experience nonetheless in the "real," the speaker makes references to outside reality:

I remember when she changed.
I could hear the far away slough of traffic
on the Brooklyn-Queens Expressway,
the people downstairs were playing salsa. (149)

However, when the spirit enters and impregnates her, she begins to take on substance, and the speaker gives birth to her. Moreover, a position is created for the skeptical reader in the speaker's roommate who represents the reality principle; she is full of disbelief and wonders about the concreteness of the spirit. The outsider-alien's remark, "humans only saw what they were told to see" comments on much of Western culture's restrictive notion of reality, which excludes dimensions of the spirit.

While the above-mentioned poems celebrate the mental transcendence of borders and boundaries, Anzaldúa also depicts the border as a material artifact to point critically to historical realities. The borderlands are implicated in the larger political sphere of U.S.-Mexico relations, which have a very real impact on the lives of its inhabitants. Natural geographic dividers such as the Rio Grande are transformed into barriers and are reinforced by human-made artifacts, demarcations that function to define national identities and to distinguish between insider and outsider.[16] Postmodern abstractions tend to ignore the political realities of barbed wire fences, the impermeability (for those from South of the border) of the Texas-Mexico border, of deportations and deaths that are the results of attempted border crossings. In a poem embedded in Anzaldúa's first essay, phrases like "gritty wire / rusted by 139 years / of the salty breath of the sea," "steel curtain," "chainlink fence crowned with rolled barbed wire" (2) stand out to stress the materiality and artificiality of the border.[17] While the Rio Grande used to be just a river, colonization has turned it into a "1,950 mile-long open wound / dividing a pueblo, a culture," which, Anzaldúa's speaker exclaims, "splits me splits me," and repeats for emphasis "*me raja me raja*" (2).

In sharp contrast to a rhetoric of celebration, Anzaldúa employs a rhetoric of violence when speaking of the border and thus clearly places her own transgressions of boundaries into a context. In her first essay, "The Homeland, Aztlán," she famously writes, "the U.S.-Mexican border *es una herida abierta* where the Third World grates against the first and bleeds" (3). While this statement experimentally traverses linguistic barriers, it nonetheless points to the material barrier and to the precarious political situation many Mexican Americans find themselves in; words like "open wound," "grates," and "bleeds" create a sense of violence and transgression and clearly contradict abstractions that are inherent in postmodern discourses. To personalize and concretize this sense of violence, Anzaldúa includes short narratives, such as the story of her cousin, a fifth-generation American citizen who, fearful and intimidated at seeing *la migra*, started running in the fields and, when found without papers, was deported.

Her poetry further problematizes the celebratory rhetoric around borders. "*El sonavabitche*" (*Borderlands* 124–29) depicts the contradictions and frequently violent tensions of living in the borderlands. The poem is a narrative of oppression and empowerment, revolving around migrant farm workers, their exploitation by farmers, and their dehumanization by the border patrol, all witnessed by the speaker of the poem. When approaching the farm, the speaker sees the *mexicanos* running from the border patrol; she

> hear[s] the shots
> ricochet off barn,
> spit into sand,
> in time to see tall men in uniforms
> thumping fists on doors
> metallic voices yelling Halt!
> their hawk eyes constantly shifting. (124)

Through staccato rhythm and drill-like lines, the voice of the poet resists dominant discourses around illegal immigration, portraying the border patrol as militaristic and robotic. Equipped with technology to enforce borders, and like inhuman predators, they hunt the *mexicanos* who are like "hares / thick limp blue-black hair / The bare heads humbly bent" (125). After listening to the story of one such migrant worker, the speaker confronts the farmer who works his migrants "from sunup to dark—15 hours a day" (127) and threatens to withhold their wages when workers refuse to show up on Sunday. When he wants to get rid of the workers, he resorts to a practice David Montejano has identified as part of "coercive labor relations," of removing wage laborers for the purpose of avoiding payment through a "timely leak" to the border patrol (197). This particular farmer, when confronted, simulates concern; he claims "how sorry he is immigration is getting so tough / a poor Mexican can't make a living / and they sure do need the work" (127). The speaker then, surprised at her own confidence, demands wages for their work: "I want two weeks wages / including two Saturdays and Sundays, / minimum wage, 15 hours a day" (127). The poem ends on a note of triumph as the speaker counts the bills the farmer hands her. This poem, an example of what Sonia Saldívar-Hull has termed Chicana resistance poetry, poetry that challenges hegemonic boundaries ("Feminism" 212; 220), reshapes and demystifies official and media discourses around illegal immigration and claims it as a necessity for the South Texas economy.

In other poems, Anzaldúa takes the favorite media phrase, of the "flood of immigrants," and gives it a human face. The dramatic monologue "*sobre piedras con lagartijos*" [On Rocks with Little Lizards; *Borderlands* 121–23][18], written entirely in Spanish, assumes a Mexican border crosser's point of view, allowing him to render the experiences of hiding in the brush in the desert in his own words. In eight stanzas, with a beginning and an ending *in medias res*, Anzaldúa presents us with a snapshot, a moment in time that both manages to reveal the man's life and his motivations for crossing, as well as to focus on the crucial moment before, presumably, being captured by the Border Patrol. Separated from his fellow-travellers, he is left with only a vague indication to proceed in a certain direction, "*ese ruido rumbo al Norte, muchachos*" [that noise toward the North, boys; all italics are in the original] (121). The first four stanzas shift back and forth between present, past, and future, as immediate observations give rise to thoughts and reflections. For instance, initial exclamations of "*Tengo que descansar, / Ay que tierra tan dura como piedra*" [I have to rest / Alas, the earth is hard as a rock] (121), lead him to reflect on the hardness/harshness of his life in Mexico, his inability to produce goods to sell at market and consequently to feed his family, his desire to earn "a few pennies" ("*unos cuantos centavos*"), and to return to his wife and children. Stanzas 6 through 8 focus on the present and future exclusively. Visible here is the speaker's increasing exhaustion, unbearable thirst, and his need to hide for days "*en la panza de ese cacto*" [in the belly of this cactus] (122) at the sound of the Border Patrol van ("*la camioneta*" 122). The poem ends abruptly with the man observing footsteps close by: "*¿De quién son esas botas / lujísimas que andan/hacia mi cara . . .?*" [Whose luxurious boots are those / Walking toward my face?] (123).

The monologue is testimony of poetry's ability to create pathos and empathy, confronting readers with the man's fear of capture, the inhospitable land he faces, and his need to search for work outside of his country. While humanizing the flood of immigrants, it simultaneously depicts the dehumanization the speaker experiences. Beginning with the title, which establishes a parallel between "wetbacks" ("*mojaditos*") and small lizards ("*lagartijos*" 121), the poem solidifies the speakers' debasement by elaborating the comparison between man and lizard. The speaker notes the similarity of their skin ("*los lagartijos y yo–tenemos el mismo cuero*" 121) and stresses that he compares unfavorably to the lizard in terms of speed ("*pero yo ya no soy ligero*" 121). Further, he notes that he is hiding like an animal ("*estoy aqui echado como animal*" 121), with the choice of the Spanish verb "echar" suggesting actions performed by dogs, for instance. He states that he will work like a donkey in the U.S. ("*yo puedo trabajar como un burro*" 121), and at the end is eye to eye with a snake, which, like the lizard, is an earth-moving creature. The poem's geographic metaphors—up/down, north/south—corroborate this theme and suggest the speaker's debasement. He is hiding, huddled up ("*me hice bola*" 122), crouching, and infantilized in the belly of the cactus, stripped of all humanity. The poem calls to task poststructuralist celebrations as well as models of globalization that stress the free flow of goods and labor by foregrounding this transnational migrant's plight.

Anzaldúa's work attests to the power of literature to act out or perform both sides of an issue; it reveals dualities and complexities. Ultimately, she pushes postmodern theorizing into new directions. Her text is an encyclopedic collection of border narratives, an inclusive enterprise. She depicts the borderlands, the space where countries meet and cultures intersect, as a site of contradictions: living on borders and in margins can be spiritually emancipating, but it is always implicated in politics and never free of conflict. Anzaldúa, true to her observation that an artist from the borderlands is "prophetically called to speech" (Hedley 36), presents us with instances of resistance to dominant culture and to idealistic or romanticizing discourses of border crossings. Her work shows the insufficiency of poststructuralist theory that forms the basis of much postmodern theorizing. "High" postmodern border rhetoric does not consider the social and economic realities at the Texas-Mexico border—the Third World squalor in which many people reside, the exorbitant crime rates, the shanty towns and maquiladoras, the environmental hazards, as well as their flipside: the border as the fountain of energy, labor, and trade. A consideration of both literal and figurative evocations of the border in Anzaldúa's text demonstrates that Chicana literature can effectively contextualize French poststructuralist theory and contribute to creating a more political version of postmodernism.

Chapter 2

Performing Identities:
Spatial Metaphors and Subjectivity in Anzaldúa, Mora, and Viramontes

> [*Nepantla* is the] Nahuatl word for the space between two bodies of water, the space between two worlds. It is a limited space, a space where you are not this or that but where you are changing. You haven't got into the new identity yet and haven't left the old identity behind either—you are in a kind of transition . . . it is very awkward, uncomfortable and frustrating to be in that *Nepantla* because you are in the midst of transformation.
>
> Gloria Anzaldúa (Ikas 237)

> If we don't know *where* we are, we have little chance of knowing *who* we are, that is if we confuse the *time* we confuse the *place;* and that when we confuse these we endanger our humanity, both physically and morally.
>
> Ralph Ellison (86)

In the preface to her edited collection *Making Face, Making Soul/Haciendo caras* Gloria Anzaldúa uses the metaphor *haciendo caras*, making faces, for the construction of Chicana identity. This identity, she claims, exists in the interfaces, the spaces "between the masks we've internalized, one on top of another . . . it is the place—the interface—between the masks that provides the space from which we can thrust out and crack the masks" (xv–xvi). Like Anzaldúa, other Chicana writers and critics situate Mexican American women through various and recurring spatial metaphors of *nepantla*, borderlands, brinks, and interstices. Chicanas speak from the "cracked spaces" (Anzaldúa, "Haciendo caras" xxii), which, according to Anzaldúa, are simultaneously the spaces of revolutionary potential (*"gestos subversivos,"* "Haciendo caras" xv).[1] Paul Jay notes how marginal spaces such as Homi Bhabha's third space, Anzaldúa's borderlands, and Mary Louise Pratt's contact zone are frequently constructed as sites from which radical revision occurs. In these oppositional spaces, Jay contends, "identities, cultures, and nations are produced, fractured, and continually reproduced"; they are "spaces where there are no fixed borders or absolutes, where previously constructed 'essences' are deployed, transformed, and reconstructed into cultural spaces whose very nature is defined by their contingency and constructedness" (169). In their emphasis on marginality and liminality, such metaphors intersect with postmodern and poststructuralist theories.

This chapter focuses on the complex intersections and interconnections between postmodern/poststructuralist theories of space and subjectivity and Chicana representations of geography and identity. As has been well documented, postmodern theories abstractly construct subjectivity as multiple and inherently unstable; I focus on the problematic use of spatial metaphors to express the dynamism of that heterogeneous subject, dispersed and multiple, through tropes of dislocation, travel, migrancy, and nomadism. Postmodern rhetoric celebrates fluidity and impermanence as expressions of the postmodern condition. The poetry and prose of Gloria Anzaldúa, Pat Mora, and Helena María Viramontes, on the other hand, help historicize these theories by showing identity in much more complex relation to specific and socially constructed geographic sites.

Since the 1960 poststructuralist and postmodern theories have challenged traditional humanist views of selfhood. They locate these views in pre-Freudian (specifically Cartesian and Enlightenment) constructions of the self as unitary, knowing, and autonomous. According to humanists, the speaking subject possesses rational control over his thoughts and actions and can claim intentionality. Since individuals develop a "core essence" from early infancy into adulthood, identity is viewed as stable and unchanging.

In contrast, poststructuralist theorists, most notably Jacques Lacan, Hélène Cixous, Julia Kristeva, and Luce Irigaray, have undertaken the dismantling of the sovereign self and replaced it with a dispersed subject. These authors build on the psychoanalysis of Freud, who proclaimed the impossibility of a unitary subject because of its basic division into two drives, the conscious and the unconscious. In his reading of Freud, Lacan goes a step further and, in his seminal essay "The Mirror Stage as Formative of the Function of the I as Revealed in Psychoanalytic Experience," declares that children's experience of wholeness as they look in the mirror and recognize themselves is illusory; he suggests that this look "manufactures for the subject, caught up in the *lure* of spatial identification, the succession of *phantasies* that extends from a fragmented body-image to a form of its *totality* that I shall call *orthopaedic*" (94; emphasis added). Simply put, then, subjectivity is non-unitary and fragmented. Poststructuralist critics indulge in a celebration of the dispersed and heterogeneous subject.[2]

Like humanist views of individualist selfhood, the notion of place has undergone a significant shift in postmodern theorizing. As Doreen Massey points out, traditionally the discipline of geography attributed stable meanings to particular places. In opposition to time, physical locations were seen as static and bounded structures (3). Literary discussions of setting frequently proceed on similar assumptions of the semantic stability of places. The setting or place can serve as a mere backdrop for the action, or it can be symbolic of the plot or the characters. Notable settings in American literature are Nathaniel Hawthorne's forests, James Fenimore Cooper's wilderness, Herman Melville's sea, or more recently, John Updike's mundane and contemporary A&P grocery store and John Cheever's suburbia. Feminist geographer Gillian Rose has pointed out that such Humanist treatments of *place* focus on the emotional responses of characters to places (41–3); they might experience the forest as haunting, for instance, or the home as a place of security and comfort.

Postmodern deconstructions contest any singular meaning attributed to "place" and expose the fabricated nature of links between places and particular significations. In contrast, Massey explains, "places are open and porous" (5), constantly subject to definition. In particular, recent theories value marginal spaces, edges, and brinks as the sites of experimentation and innovation and as privileged spaces from which Western philosophy can be critiqued. For example, psychoanalytic materialists Gilles Deleuze and Félix Guattari use the spatial metaphor of territorialization to suggest Western culture's tendency towards homogeneous organizational groupings as in nation, church, family, etc. They suggest a strategy of "deterritorialization" to counter this tendency and to enable oppositional knowledges. In *Kafka: Toward a Minor Literature*, they declare the latter as the space of Kafka's art. As a Czech Jew writing in German, Kafka produced a "minor" literature that challenged existing hierarchies of knowledge. To describe his deterritorialized work, they use the botanical metaphor of the rhizome, an "acentered, nonhierarchical, nonsignifying system without a General and without an organizing memory or central automaton" (Deleuze and Guattari, *A Thousand* 21). They advocate this strategy for anyone willing to achieve oppositional consciousness.

Poststructuralist discourses usefully dislodge notions of stable centers, places, and identities, and show the discursive construction of subjectivites and spaces.

However, as many critics have pointed out, their blind spot is an ahistoricity and insufficient regard of power relations. For Lacan "spatial identification" (94) means nothing more than looking in the mirror to determine one's wholeness, but, as Diana Fuss suggests, in Lacanian positionality the place of the subject is "ultimately, unlocalizable" (30). What is at stake, then, when the nomad/migrant becomes a privileged figure of destabilization and alterity? Or, in Caren Kaplan's words, "When the first world critics advocate a process of 'becoming minor' it is necessary to ask: . . . What are we losing with such a move? What do we stand to gain? . . . I would have to pay attention to whether or not it is possible for me to *choose* deterritorialization or whether deterritorialization has chosen me" ("Deterritorialization" 191). In *Questions of Travel: Postmodern Discourses of Displacement* Kaplan rigorously critiques the celebration and the "aestheticized tendencies of poststructuralist nomadologies and theories of displacement in Euro-American modernist and postmodern thought" (130). She argues that it is founded on the privileged figures of postmodern/postcolonial emigrés whose detachment from their home location leads to aesthetic productivity. She further shows how these tropes are implicated in anti-feminist and colonial sentiments and fail to account for the transnational power relations that construct postmodern subjectivities.[3]

A look at migration patterns gives valuable insight into the historical displacements and disjunctures many Mexican Americans have experienced. It may counter postmodern ahistoricity and ground spatial metaphors in Chicana fiction. It also shows that movement is not random but constricted by social and economic patterns. The annexation of Northern Mexican territories by the U.S. in 1848 resulted in various displacements and South/North migrations. Jorge Durand, Douglass S. Massey, and Fernando Charvet discuss four phases of what they call the changing geography of Mexican immigration to the U.S.: first, *the classic era* of open migration before the restrictive policies of the 1920s, which included massive labor displacements during the regime of Porfirio Díaz; second, *the Bracero era* of 1942–64, when the U.S. sponsored a large temporary worker program after a wave of mass deportations during the Great Depression; third, the *era of undocumented migration*, spanning the time between the end of the Bracero Program and the passage of the Immigration Reform and Control Act of 1986 (IRCA); and fourth, the *post-IRCA era* from 1987 to the present, during which time the government has sought to suppress undocumented migration—some of it triggered through the peso devaluation of 1994— through increasingly repressive actions (2). Anthropologist Roger Rouse further explores the most recent migration patterns in his essay "Mexican Migration and the Social Space of Postmodernism" and specifically links these patterns to spatial metaphors. Based on his study of townspeople from rural Aguililla in the state of Michoacán, he challenges theories of unidirectional migration and suggests that in a transnational economy, traditional spatial metaphors such as those of community and center/periphery, must be replaced by new images of border and circuit. The border image better accounts for "the chronic maintenance of two quite distinct ways of life" (14), and that of the circuit illustrates frequently circular migrations, as well as the "circulation of people, money, goods, and information" (14).

Chicanas' use of geographical metaphors and tropes of nomadism and migrancy intersects to a significant degree with recent postmodern and poststructuralist theoretizations of difference, otherness, and alterior spaces, and in fact precedes them.[4] A close examination of the works of Anzaldúa, Mora, and Viramontes reveals that this migratory sensibility finds expression not just in the prevalence of spatial metaphors but also in the multivocality of Chicana texts: the generic hybridity of Anzaldúa's work, the polyvocality of Mora's poetry, and the multiple shifting points of view in Viramontes's novel. However, these works problematize the lack of historical specificity in much contemporary theoretical rhetoric. These writers claim marginal spaces and resignify them into spaces of power. But they also show that speaking from the interfaces, as Anzaldúa explains in the above epigraph, exacts a toll. Her book most directly engages with the multiplicity of the postmodern subject and shows that as the space of intercultural encounter, the borderlands sometimes painfully forge mestiza identity; Mora uses liminal spaces as metaphors for social location and concrete class conflicts among Chicanas; and Viramontes enacts the most stringent critique of postmodern celebration of nomadism and migrancy by pointing out the material and economic limits of the mobility.

What has been called a "new geographics of identity" helps provide a more historically specific framework for the relations between space and subjectivity. As defined by Susan Stanford Friedman, this term captures the new identity studies that centralize space. It challenges traditional models of narrative that privilege time by focusing not on "ordered movement of linear growth but the lack of solid ground, the ceaseless change of fluidity" (19). In this articulation, *space* (in contrast to place) as a geopolitical category is related to identity; physical location is one among many axes through which identities are constituted.[5] Space, in this conceptualization, is related to culture and to the social; space is a setting for social interactions and site of relations of power. As Friedman suggests, "Space often functions as a trope for cultural location—for identity and knowledge as locationally as well as historically produced. Setting works as symbolic geography, signaling or marking the specific cultural location of a character within the larger society" (137). Spatial narratives, then, inscribe and critique histories and power relations. Mary Pat Brady emphasizes this point in her discussion of Sandra Cisneros's short story collection *Women Hollering Creek*. She states that "no place exists apart from the social interactions that construct it or the discursive systems that elaborate it" (129).[6]

The historical production of connections between space and identity might become clearer when looking at how American spaces have been discursively constructed in the past. The U.S. American West, for instance, has intricately been connected both to shaping *national* as well as *individual* identities. Westward expansion was linked to ideas of manifest destiny; the virgin land, the wilderness was to be conquered. St. John de Crèvecoeur writes in 1782 that the West is populated by "industrious people, who . . . will change in a few years that hitherto barbarous country into a fine fertile, well-regulated district" (15–16). For Frederick Jackson Turner the space of the West becomes a constitutive force in the creation of individualist identities: "To the frontier American intellect owes its striking characteristics: coarseness and strength combined with acuteness and inquisitiveness, and a practical, inventive turn of mind" (27). Turner's pioneer, the rugged individualist, becomes part of popular mythology.

This spatialization of national and individual identities has marginalized Mexican American Others, who were constructed as part of this wild terrain and conquerable territory. Gloria Anzaldúa quotes Texas historian (and agitator for independence from Mexico) William H. Wharton, who writes similarly (as de Crèvecoeur and Turner) of the Southern frontier but with a distinct sense of racial superiority:

> The justice and benevolence of God will forbid that . . . Texas should again become a howling wilderness trod only by savages, or . . benighted by the ignorance and superstition, the anarchy and rapine of Mexican misrule. The Anglo-American race are destined to be forever the proprietors of this land of promise and fulfillment. . . . Their flocks range its boundless pastures, for them its fertile lands will yield . . . luxuriant harvests . . The wilderness of Texas has been redeemed by Anglo-American blood & enterprise. (Anzaldúa, *Borderlands* 7)

Note the contrast in both Wharton and de Crèvecoeur between the Romantic ideal of the howling wilderness and the Neo-Classicist ideal of an organized, harmonious, and pastoral landscape suggested by images of "boundless pastures" and "fertile lands." Such discussions show the implications of topographical descriptions in ideological formations and the power relations of territorial conquest.[7]

The Chicano movement has created its own symbolic geography in juxtaposition to these spatial constructions, most importantly Aztlán, that spiritual homeland of the Mexica people located in the southwestern United States. Chicano critic Rafael Pérez-Torres explains that Aztlán is the land of seven caves, place of the Twisted Hill, from which the Mexica migrated southward in 820 AD. This cultural imaginary is invoked in "El plan espiritual de Aztlán" (1969), one of the manifestos of the Chicano movement and its declaration of independence. The plan states:

> In the spirit of a new people that is conscious not only of its proud historical heritage, but also of the brutal "gringo" invasion of our territories, we, the Chicano inhabitants and civilizers of the northern land of Aztlán, from whence came our forefathers, reclaiming the land of their birth and consecrating the determination of our pope of the sun, declare that the call of our blood is our power, our responsibility, and our inevitable destiny. (Valdez and Steiner 402–3)

The writers of the plan profess ownership of the land and base their entitlement on pre-Cortesian history. Chicano/a writers too have evoked Aztlán as an icon of cultural unity and envision the Southwest as "la santa tierra" (Rebolledo, "Tradition" 96), as the land that nourishes, that represents traditional family ties, that provides strength. A sampling of Pat Mora's poetry titles reveals this preoccupation with the land, "Desert Women," "Mi Madre," or "Mi Tierra."

However, nationalist yearnings for Aztlán tend to construct Chicano/a identity as static and unitary, anchored in one location. Since the 1980s, a different spatialization has gained currency, that of the borderlands, which, according to Pérez-Torres, serves as metaphor, emblem, and reality of Chicano/a identity (*Movements* 156). The borderlands are "the contact zone," the place where cultures intersect, where languages are mixed, where mestiza identities are created. According to Anzaldúa's famous definition, "the borderlands are present whenever two or more cultures edge each other, where people of different races occupy the same territory, where under, lower, middle and upper classes touch, where the space between individuals shrinks with intimacy" (*Borderlands,* "Preface").[8] For José David Saldívar the border zone is a paradigm of crossings, intercultural exchanges, circulations, resistances, and negotiations (*Border Matters* ix). The borderlands create *mestizaje*, identities that are syncretic products of these multiple and various encounters. Anzaldúa's borderlands are both literal geographic sites and also metaphoric conditions that bespeak Chicana identity.

As a Chicana lesbian, Anzaldúa is doubly displaced. Her sexuality leads to her expulsion from home, and her ethnicity to a migratory lifestyle. The structure of her borderlands narrative begins and ends in the private space of "home." Gillian Rose explains that Humanist geography has constructed home as a place of attachments; she says that in Y.-F. Tuan's famous theory, the "hearth, shelter, home or home base are intimate places to human beings everywhere;" home is "that special place to which one withdraws and from which on [sic] ventures forth;" it is ultimately "a field of care" (Rose 47). These significations are often found in literature as well. Anzaldúa uses such traditional constructions of home when she speaks metaphorically of language as a homeland and of her home tongues being not one but many (*Borderlands* 56), or when she talks about tribal cultures keeping art work in the home and not in public places (68). In one of her lyrical evocations of her homeland she writes, "There are more subtle ways that we internalize identification, especially in the forms of images and emotions. For me food and certain smells are tied to my identity, to my homeland. Woodsmoke curling up to an immense blue sky; woodsmoke perfuming my grandmother's clothes, her skin . . ." (61). Here home, the literal geographic site, is clearly the place of emotional attachments.

However, as feminist critics such as Doreen Massey or Minnie Bruce Pratt have shown, for many women home is a contested site.[9] Frequently, home is a social space that reproduces patriarchal structures. Noncompliance with these norms leads to dislocation. In Anzaldúa's narrative, home is also an impediment to growth. Despite the above-mentioned positive valuations of "home," Anzaldúa uses the trope of exile, of being cast out of her homeland (80). Home has become a hostile environment because she rebels against patriarchal strictures. As a Chicana lesbian she feels like an alien and states, "to this day I'm not sure where I found the strength to leave the source, my mother, disengage from my family, *mi tierra, mi gente* . . . I had to leave home so I could find myself" (16). Her student's misunderstanding of "homophobia" as a "fear of going home," expressing her exclusion by her community (20–1), perfectly illustrates Anzaldúa's contentious description of this space.

Anzaldúa's involuntary move from home, however, is not expressed through horizontal movement across space. An exile, she travels to seek refuge in spiritual connections instead, and these connections are signified by the trope of the underground, an imaginary, non-hegemonic space.[10] Her spiritual guide and mentor is Coatlicue, serpent goddess of the Aztecs. Assuming the Coatlicue state means letting go of rationality and seeking different layers of meaning and modes of perception. In this vertical movement, described in the book as a "plunge" that contains its own risks, transformations take place: "The work takes place underground—subconsciously. It is work that the soul performs" (79). As I have shown in chapter one, in poems such as "Poets Have Strange Eating Habits" and "Protean Being" this transformatory search for depth is expressed in tunneling images (39; 43).

While the journey inward signifies an encounter with the self, the borderlands appear in Anzaldúa's narrative as the sites of intercultural encounters and palimpsestic migrations. She begins her book with a section entitled "The Lost Land," which narrates the various voluntary and coerced North-South and South-North migrations, of the Aztecs, of European Americans, and of Mexicans (4, 6). This multiply traversed space of the borderlands contains, like a palimpsest, remnants of all of these cultures. The identity forged in this cauldron is that of the *mestiza*, and her existence resides *en la encrucijada* [the crossroads] (80), *en los intersticiones* [the spaces between the different worlds she inhabits] (20), and in the interface (38). Through spatial metaphors such as these, Anzaldúa specifies the location of *mestizaje* in the margins, between cracks and fissures, and eliding stable categories. She writes, "I sit between warmth and cold never knowing which is my territory" (50).

The political urgency invested in Anzaldúa's vision, which she significantly calls a "validation vision," differs sharply from poststructuralist representations of *mestizaje*. French philosopher Jean Luc Nancy, for instance, in a move similar to Deleuze and Guattari's, appropriates and decontextualizes *mestizaje*. In the "Postscriptum" to his essay "Cut Throat Sun" he asks, " Isn't it already going too far to talk about *mestizaje*? As if *mestizaje* were 'some thing,' a substance, an object, an identity (an identity!) that could be grasped and 'processed'" (122). Instead, *mestizaje* is a general condition in which he (along with everyone else) partakes as a "*mestizo* of Spanish and Viking, of Celt and Roman, and more importantly: of *je-ne-sais-quois*" (123). We must consider "the *mestizaje* of identity itself," he claims (121). This discussion emphasizes the ludic activity *mestizaje* enables–"a mestizo is someone who is on the border, on the very border of *meaning*" (123)—and de-emphasizes the specific historical conditions of Chicanos/as.[11]

In her prose piece "El camino de la mestiza/ the mestiza way" (82-3) Anzaldúa outlines a road map for mestizas, a utopian vision cast in geographic language. Here Anzaldúa reclaims marginal and alterior sites as spaces of power, and she does so through subversive gestures that demand a new consciousness, a mestiza consciousness. The mestiza's location in *nepantla*, Nahua word for the land in the middle, speaks to her ability to navigate her territory and to straddle borders—"We are on both shores at once" (78). Due to this flexibility, the mestiza learns "divergent thinking" (79). This "conscious rupture" (82) leads to a transcendence of dualities, and from this position, the mestiza is able to

> reinterpret history and, using new symbols, she shapes new myths. She adopts new perspectives toward the darkskinned, women and queers. She strengthens her tolerance (and intolerance) for ambiguity. She is willing to share, to make herself vulnerable to foreign ways of seeing and thinking. She surrenders all notions of safety, of the familiar. Deconstruct, construct. She becomes a *nahual*, able to transform herself. . . . (82-3)

The mestiza thus claims agency in form of the power of (re)definition and through her role as mediator: "I gather the splintered and disowned parts of *la gente mexicana* and hold them in my arms. *Todas las partes de nosotros valen*" (85).

The poem "To live in the borderlands means you" from the corresponding poetry section of the book supplements these themes of empowerment by illustrating the insecurities that reside in this *mestizaje*.

> To live in the Borderlands means you
> are neither *hispana india negra española*
> *ni gabacha, eres mestiza, mulata,* half-breed
> caught in the crossfire between camps
> while carrying all five races on your back
> not knowing which side to turn to, run from; (194)

The borderlands in this poem is one of violent intercultural encounter. The speaker's internalization of the spatial metaphors, according to which the battleground lies within oneself, illustrates the painful nature of this encounter. Thus, the mestiza is caught between two sides and wards off attacks from both:

> In the Borderlands
> you are the battleground
> where enemies are kin to each other;
> you are at home, a stranger, the border disputes have been settled
> the volley of shots have shattered the truce

you are wounded, lost in action
dead, fighting back. (194)

The poem's conclusion with its images of borderlessness and crossroads suggests the mestiza's location:

To survive in the Borderlands
you must live *sin fronteras*
be a crossroads. (195)

Like Hermes Trismegistos, Greek messenger from the Gods, *mestizaje* resides at the intersection of two ways, on the border of two worlds. Like Hermes the trickster, the mestiza's constant negotiations involve craft and cunning.

As the borderlands form a third country, mestiza identity, according to Anzaldúa, is a new species as well. Both Anzaldúa and Mora use the term *nepantla,* which metaphorically illustrates the space Chicanas inhabit: they are the people of that middle country, torn between conflicting ways of life. The person in the middle, who simultaneously suffers from and is empowered by cultural schizophrenia, inhabits *nepantla*. Pat Mora writes about the complex and ongoing negotiations of identity in her collection of essays:

> I am a child of the border, that land corridor bordered by the two countries that have most influenced my perception of reality. . . There probably isn't a week of my life that I don't have at least one experience when I feel that discomfort, that slight frown from someone that wordlessly asks, What is someone like her doing here? But I am in the middle of my life, and well know not only the pain but also the advantage of observing both sides, albeit with my own biases, of moving through two, and, in fact, multiple spaces, and selecting from both what I want to make part of me, of consciously shaping my space. (*Nepantla* 5-6)[12]

Mora explores *nepantla* and living on both sides in slightly different ways from Anzaldúa, specifically by linking geographic and *social* locations. Based on the idea that identities are multiple and relational, her poetry explores the social location of her speakers—middle class women—and their relations to other Mexican American women. Her spatial imagery calls attention to the unequal social relations among women that is expressed and constituted through spatial differentiation (Rose 113). She thereby engages in a politics of location. Originating with Adrienne Rich, the politics of location represents the awareness of the hierarchical differences among women,[13] specifically European American feminists and women of color. Mora's poems, in contrast, explore power differences among Mexican

American women.

The poem "Sonrisas" from the collection *Borders* begins with a statement of one such speaker's physical location: "I live in a doorway/ between two rooms" (20), a location that captures her precarious positioning between two worlds. She continues to elaborate the contrast between the two rooms: the one a conference room in which academic women in suits talk about curriculum, tenure, and budget, and the other a room where custodians share gossip in Spanish. The observer in the doorway is part of the middle class professionals, yet she feels like an alien among them, and her allegiance clearly belongs to the custodians: the gossip, the whirling laughter are sharply contrasted with the professionals' "quick, beige smiles/that seldom sneak into their eyes" (20) and represent the zone of comfort. What seems set up as a binary opposition between inhabitants of two worlds—European American and Mexican American—in fact serves, as Teresa McKenna points out, as an anti-essentialist move: the speaker does not stand between them but permanently "lives" between. McKenna continues, the poet lives in suspension and "does not locate herself in either world" (120).

Thus in Mora's poem, it is the more privileged person who voluntarily lives in the margins. The poem "Echoes," also from *Borders*, represents a similar conflict, narrated through spatial imagery. Here the speaker, a mother at a children's birthday party, "sipped white wine/with the women in cool dresses/ and sculptured nails" (23) and then joins the Mexican maid inside who secretly wonders why she'd leave the company and speak with her in Spanish. By entering the house, the speaker has "drift[ed] to the edge," the space on the margins the Mexican maid inhabits, and joins her to observe middle class values from this viewpoint. The speaker's association with the maid in fact constitutes an indictment of the other women's attitudes, carelessly tossing candy and colored paper on the ground and telling their guests to "just drop the cups and plates/ on the grass. My maid/ will pick them up." It depicts the new locations for wealthy women: outside in the garden, while the traditionally female space of the kitchen, the place they have vacated, is now inhabited by ethnic minorities. The speaker, in effect, crosses class barriers by choosing to help the maid set the table. All the while she thinks of the rebellion of the land to such abuse:

> I longed to hear this earth
> roar, to taste thunder,
> to see proper smiles twist
> as those black words echoed

in the wind again and again:
just drop . . . my maid
just drop . . .
my maid.

Through the poem's multivocality, its iteration, "echoes," or snippets of the others' speech, the speaker is called upon to resist such attitudes:

Perhaps my desert land waits
to hear me roar, waits to hear
me flash: NO. NO.
Again and again. (*Borders* 23–24)

These poems point to the many divisions among women along the axes of gender, ethnicity, and class. In an interview with Norma Alarcón, Pat Mora has stated that the border area

> forces one to see the problems of people facing serious economic hardships. You cannot live in El Paso and not see that. Whether you are one of the fortunate ones who has a nice *señora* coming to help you with your housework, or something else, these people become part of your life. You hear their stories. When I drive to work to the University (of Texas, at El Paso), I see their houses right across the river. So, every day I am aware of the differences between my life and theirs, and of the role of chance in one's life. I could have been born on the other side of the river. (121)

Mora's speakers move to the margins to side with the disempowered and thus become permanent travelers between worlds.

In her 1995 novel *Under the Feet of Jesus,* Viramontes most directly confronts theories of the nomadic postmodern subject by critiquing the material and economic limits of mobility. In contrast to poststructuralist theories of nomadism and migrancy, Viramontes presents a very un-idyllic picture of migrant workers in Southern California by providing a topography of the state little known in American fiction, a California of urban barrios and rural labor camps. The topography intersects with history in recalling the grape pickers strikes in the 1960s and 70s, César Chávez's work, and the exploitative conditions at large agro companies. Viramontes symbolically evokes this connection with casual references to the flyers workers find one day that flaunt the symbol of the black eagle. At the center of the novel is a family of migrant workers whose unending movements, voluntary and involuntary, across space are carefully constrained and scripted. The novel shows the connections between a postmodern transnational economy, movement of labor, and geographic spaces. Petra, her oldest daughter Estrella (the novel's protagonist), and her siblings are not postcolonial emigrés, for whom the pleasure of perpetual oscillation between locations leads to a fluid and all-incorporating identity. Instead, by presenting us with images of rural poverty in the midst of the "land of plenty," Viramontes shows how local and private spaces are implicated in larger geopolitical issues.

At the beginning of *Under the Feet of Jesus*, Petra "refolded the Phillips 66 map" (4), as her family arrives with Petra's companion, Perfecto Flores, at their new place of work in an unspecified labor camp in Southern California. This arrival and its suggestion of stasis traditionally presents the endpoint of narratives: a goal has been reached, and obstacles have been overcome to reach this goal. In this novel, however, everything is provisional and temporary: arrivals, departures, places, communities, and subjectivities. Throughout the novel, Viramontes dislodges common associations we have of stasis and movement to demonstrate the vital importance of these concepts for this Mexican American family.

Viramontes's novel provides a postmodern topography in its deconstruction of traditional concepts of spaces as static and bounded structures. Spaces in this novel do not have fixed significations but are always in the process of construction. They are multiply inscribed, defined, and redefined. The narrator hints at this semantic instability at the very beginning of the novel: "The silence and the clouds and the barn meant many things" (4). Like the mercury Estrella sees at a nurse's station, which is simultaneously "Metallic and liquid. Solid and diffused" (141), spaces are contradictory. Viramontes's technique of multiple selective omniscience further enhances the fluidity and provisionality of each definition. For example, the first edifice the family encounters, the barn, serves as focal point and landmark that functions as the children's orientation to their new environment. The first few lines of the novel present Estrella's perspective of the structure: "Had they been heading for the barn all along ? . . . The barn had burst through a clearing of trees and the cratered roof reminded her of the full moon" (3). The barn is constructed here as the ultimate goal of their journey. As the narrative progresses, Estrella comes to see it as a "cathedral of a building" (9). Like a cathedral, the barn offers her sanctuary when she escapes there from the midday heat. It is also inhabited by birds, symbols of flight, and provides the setting for a momentary transformative idyll. In the middle of the novel, after her first sexual experience, Estrella runs to the barn, and amid the "musk hot scent of manure" (89) and the cobwebs, "the safety pins on the cuffs of her sleeves glimmered like diamonds" (90). The tension between "manure" and "diamonds" illustrates the multiple and contradictory meanings ascribed to the edifice, which assumes additional meanings through the perspectives of other characters. Thus adults warn the children not to go there because of its dilapidated state. It is also the site where a deformed child appears and a death has taken place. Finally, for Perfecto the barn assumes yet a different signification: he wants to tear it down for the landowners and sees it as a way to make money so he can embark on his journey home.

Other spaces in the novel are similarly multidimensional. The family of seven finds its future home down the mud road in what they euphemistically call a "bungalow," a two-room shack. Its warped steps lead to a shabby wood frame, and the inside of a dingy room, divided from the other with a blanket, "stink[s] of despair" (8). There are no sanitary facilities and "no beds," only "a few crates used for chairs arranged around one table as if for a game of cards" (8). These words define the bungalow as a space of temporary habitation; they suggest the presence of previous tenants and the constant coming and going of people. Through her housekeeping endeavors, Petra nonetheless makes this space their home. Upon arrival, she notes, "The grate needed scrubbing, and she looked around for horsetail weed, which was just as good for scouring as steelwool" (7). By cleaning, she erases the tracks of previous inhabitants; by setting up her altar, she gives this space a center; and by drawing the lines around the house to ward off intrusion of scorpions, she makes this space secure for the family. Petra redefines this space as home; wherever she goes, she demonstrates her ability to create spaces, showing her flexibility and strength.

Other spaces that are part of the family's rural environment are destabilized through dramatic irony and the juxtaposition of perspectives. From the children's point of view, the irrigation ditch provides particular pleasure. They are drawn to this space for its "clear cool water" and velvety waves. However, the ditch is poisoned by pesticides, and one day while reading comic books, Estrella and a friend see a drowned, bloated dog floating down the canal. On a larger scale, the novel also recalls and then demystifies Chicano constructions of Mexican Americans' ties to the land and romantic idealizations of Aztlán. On the one hand, Petra claims ownership of the land which figures as "mother" and evokes the Plan of Aztlán by telling Estrella, when the girl fears the border patrol, "Tell them Que tienes una madre aquí. You are not an orphan, and she pointed a red finger to the earth, Aquí" (63). But the earth the piscadores work on is also an inhospitable place. The monotony of the vast, silent, and endless fields is oppressive (50); they are exposed to the hot soil on which they toil and to the scorching sun, which provokes fainting spells and drains them. The Aztec symbol of the "white sun so mighty" is quickly demystified as it "toasted the green grapes to black raisins" (50).

Associative flashbacks take Estrella to the city apartment, which at first suggested a more sedentary lifestyle and stable place of residence: "They settled in a city apartment with the hope of never seeing another labor camp again" (13). But the potential the apartment offers is deconstructed through its location just underneath a freeway exchange. With the constant fear of cars crashing through the window, this location offers a very un-idyllic view of home and domesticity. The apartment remains a temporary abode; as they are still settling in, the father's abandonment forces them to move on. Estrella remembers all the subsequent moves, "all night packing with trash bags left behind, to a cheaper rent they couldn't afford, to Estrella's godmother's apartment, to some friends, finally to the labor camps again. Always leaving things behind that they couldn't fit, couldn't pack, couldn't take like a trail of bread crumbs for her father" (14).

As the novel shows the discursive construction of spaces, it also demonstrates how movement and mobility are circumscribed and governed by strict rules. First, movement is gendered. Men have a greater degree of freedom of mobility than do women, as is evidenced by Estrella's father's desertion and Perfecto's desire to leave. Men own the means of mobility, cars, and what little money there is. However, the novel further uses the technique of ironic juxtaposition and contrast to show mobility as tied to economic reality. Two main symbols illustrate this point. One is the train, which represents escape and lures the field workers with constant movement and promise of flight. The piscadores, heads earth-bound, collectively stop "to listen to the freight train rattling along the tracks swiftly, its horn sounding like the pressing of an accordion. The lone train broke the sun and silence with its growing thunderous roar and the train reminded the piscadores of destinations, arrivals and departures, of home and not of home" (55). Cars carry similar symbolic weight. While Perfecto's old Chevy Capri station wagon, with its broken muffler, cracked dashboard, and perpetually empty gas tank, will not carry the family very far, it is sharply contrasted with the lime green Bermuda with a white top and white wall tires that Estrella sees at a gas station. In this flashback, Estrella and her siblings have to cross a dangerous highway to get to the gas station's grocery store, and Estrella longingly eyes the Bermuda parked there. The car is a symbol of a different world whose owner, she imagines, "could travel from one splat dot to another. She thought him a man who knew his neighbors well, who returned to the same bed, who could tell where the schools and where the stores were, and where Nescafé coffee jars in the stores were located, and payday always the same at the end of the week" (105). In contrast, as Petra is tediously traveling by foot, she reflects, "[she] knew the capricious black lines on a map did little to reveal the hump and tear of the stitched pavement which ascended to the morning sun and through the trees and no trees" (103). In the same way, then, the road serves as a contradictory image, conjuring up moments of Kerouacian idealizations of freedom and deflating them.

These contrasts point to social inequities and stress Estrella's family's slow, carefully controlled movement through space. The freedom invoked through trains and cars serves to highlight the lack of freedom of movement of Estrella's family. Travel and tourism are clearly not possibilities. The following interchange between Alejo and Estrella explores the tensions between mobility and settlement, both equally desirable but equally ambiguous. Alejo begins,

—If we don't have oil, we don't have gasoline.
—Good. We'd stay put then.
—Stuck, more like it. Stuck.
—Aren't we now? (86).

The characters' sense of being stuck is expressed in the image of bound feet (87) and narrativized later on in the novel when on the way to the nurse's station to get help for Alejo, who had fallen ill from being sprayed by a biplane, the car gets stuck on the road, its tires endlessly spinning. Estrella tries to build a road with rocks, unsuccessfully at first, but she keeps paving and repaving (130). At the end of the afternoon, on their way home, the empty gas tank again represents stalled movement.

Other geographical markers indicate the controlled and patrolled spaces that confine the family's movement and perfectly illustrate urban historian Mike Davis's description of postmodern California in terms of a "proliferation of new repressions in space and movement" (quoted in Saldívar, *Border Matters* 6). JoAnn Pavletich and Margot Gayle Backus's suggestion concerning Viramontes's short stories is equally pertinent here: "Viramontes's characters negotiate restrictive and unstable terrain" (135). Wherever they go, fences limit movement, whether it be the corral around their camp, which workers redesignate as the place for socializing, or "thistle thorns that were planted around the fenceless edges of the orchards to discourage roadside thievery" (103), or "the lopping wire fence" guarded by a watchdog (107). There is also the controlled movement back and forth from the fields on trucks. Here the picadores are "herded out of the corralled flatbed," complete with iron-bolted doors, and, during their transport, "bumped into one another like loose change in a pocket" (67). Moreover, since deportation is an ever-present threat to their existences, the characters keep their immigration papers under the feet of the statue of Jesus in the bungalow. Estrella experiences this fear one night as she walks back to the camp along the railroad tracks. She lingers a while and sits on the tracks to watch a baseball game. Her vision is blurred; it is twilight, and a tall wire mesh fence separates the tracks from the ball field, indicating a separation of worlds. When suddenly she sees headlights, which she attributes to the border patrol, "[s]he tried to remember which side she was on and which side of the wire mesh she was safe in" (60). Viramontes brilliantly superimposes four scenes on top of one another, which all function to distort reality: there is, on the most literal level, the baseball game, representing the all-American past time. But on the other hand, the baseball is transformed in Estrella's mind into the peach, a valuable commodity she had wanted to save but was compelled to give away to a toothless old man earlier that day. Watching the children carelessly playing in the ballpark, she thinks, "Who would catch the peach, who was hungry enough to run the field in all that light?" (60). Two other scenes are grafted onto this one: one evokes an encounter at the border, complete with fence and floodlight and the fear (for Mexican immigrants) of violence. As the ball hits the bat, it becomes, in Estrella's mind, "a blunt instrument against a skull" (60). This triggers the comparison to a hunting scene, where the immigrant becomes a "stunned deer waiting for a bullet" (60). Through free association, Estrella shows how topographical descriptions are implicated in historical relations of power.

Such power relations, Viramontes shows, have a direct impact on the human body. The novel employs stark metaphors of space that connect geographical spaces with the geography of human bodies. As Anzaldúa explains, "'Face' is the surface of the body that is most noticeably inscribed by social structures, marked with instincts on how to be mujer . . . working class, Chicana. As mestizas, we have different surfaces for each identity" ("Haciendo caras" xv). Viramontes advances a similar materialist feminist aesthetics: the body, and not just the face, is important for subjectivity since bodies are inscribed by social structures. The bodies of the piscadores are written on, marked, and scarred. Emerging from the field they appear as "a patch quilt of people charred by the sun: brittle women with bandannas over their noses, their salt-and pepper hair dusted brown . . . and men so old they were thought to be dead when they slept" (57). The narrative pays much attention to the frailty of Perfecto's and Petra's bodies. Their bodies suggest a scarred landscape, a wasteland. Thus Perfecto's hands "were too big for such a wiry body, with veins that surfaced like swollen roots" (73); there are "thin stray hairs in the valley of his armpit" (115); in a dream he sees his veins "like irrigation canals clogged with dying insects" (100); and as he bends "his wiry limbs, an old weathervane of a body, the rusted axis of his knees [is] rattling like pivots in the wind" (78). Repeatedly, descriptions of Petra's body center on her varicose veins, which are "[l]ike vines choking the movement of her legs" (61); they "ruptured like earthquake fault lines" (124). Inversely, physical spaces are mapped in terms of the human body as well: for instance, the railroad ties look, to Estrella, "like the stitches of the mother's caesarean scar as far as her eyes could see" (59), referring to sex-specific scarrings through childbirth.

Through broken bodies and imposed identities, Viramontes's subaltern characters struggle to achieve a sense of self-worth, subjectivity, and agency. Repeatedly bombarded with symbols of American subjectivity, Estrella constantly confronts what she is not: visible to her teachers like her fellow students, beautiful like the nurse, well-off like the man in the Bermuda. The few encounters with European Americans staged in the novel are telling in the ways in which they interpellate Estrella's subjectivity. For example, Estrella meets with indifference and racism at school where the last rows are always reserved for migrant children, and where teachers are more concerned with the dirt under her nails than with answering her questions. The nurse to whom they take Alejo doesn't really grasp their plight; her life is evoked through her perfect makeup and perfume, and the images of her beautiful children on her desk while Estrella stands in front of her in a dirty dress.

To counter his sense of anonymity and invisibility, Alejo displaces it onto the images of a boulder and a tarpit, geographical metaphors that here represent *psychic* terrain. To reassure himself of the reality of his existence, he keeps a rock in his pocket. "He loved stones and the history of stones because he believed himself to be a solid mass of boulder thrust out of the earth and not some particle lost in infinite and cosmic space" (52). Contrasting with the solidity of the stone is the image of the tarpits and his fear of sinking into them. At the turning point in his narrative, when he hears the pesticide planes approaching, "he closed his eyes and imagined sinking into the tar pits" (78). He imagines the tar engulfing him, and sinking deeper, he sees "thousands of bones, the bleached white marrow made a whole, surfaced bone. No fingerprint or history, bone. No lavae stone. No story or family, bone" (78). The tar pits are full of anonymous bones, the collective resting place of the invisible. When the family's car later gets stuck, and mud reaches her knees, Estrella recalls the story Alejo told her about the bones of a girl found in the La Brea tar pits: "They found her in a few bones. No details of her life were left behind, no piece of cloth, no ring, no doll" (129).

On the one hand, the tar pits serve as the perfect expression of the migrants' condition: they have no geographical anchors or stable locations for identity. But on the other hand, they serve as a devastating social commentary on the political system where labor is invisible, underground, a mass of unidentified bones, incinerated to fuel the American economy. As Paul Lauter writes about Bertolt Brecht's "A Worker Reads History," "workers of the world have been hidden from history" (838). Estrella connects this cluster of images communicated to her by Alejo and relates it specifically to her family's social and economic situation: "She remembered the tar pits. Energy money, the fossilized bones of energy matter. How bones made oil and oil made gasoline. The oil was made from their bones, and it was their bones that kept the nurse's car from not halting on some highway, kept her on her way to Daisyfield to pick up her boys at six. It was their bones that kept the air conditioning in the cars humming . . . Their bones" (148).

Estrella clearly makes a mark in her climactic act of resistance when she brings down the crowbar on the nurse's desk to get the family's gas money back. But does this act not seem to elevate her to a position of heroic individualism? Is the novel an emblem of female individualist self-assertion? Does Viramontes "lapse into individualism," a phenomenon that is, according to Ellen McCracken, quite common in recent Latina literature (66)? This position would seem to find support in two significant scenes, one depicting Estrella as she emerges through the hospital doors after dropping off Alejo, where she appears to her siblings as Moses parting the red sea. The second takes place, once again, in the barn. In contrast to the snake the family saw crushed in the road—a symbol of their own contingency in the traffic of the world—Estrella appears in this final scene as the Virgin of Guadalupe who steps on serpents to express her dominion over them. The Virgen de Guadalupe imagery helps declare Estrella as an agent of resistance, as the Virgin was the universally adopted symbol of resistance during the farm workers' strikes. Cecilia Lawless would concur in her argument that Estrella has the power to be a beacon of hope rather than falling into disrepair like the barn, "Homeless," Lawless writes, "even within her domestic spheres, this woman will become, I contend, a builder engaged in establishing strong foundations for future homes" (378).

As an alternative, I offer a reading of the final scene where subjectivities, like buildings, are makeshift; significant actions occur only through "micropolitical agencies," as de Lauretis explains in *Technologies of Gender*, not foundational assumptions of individualism. In the midst of the dilapidated barn, which readers have seen stripped of its glamor, Estrella's moment of triumph remains a temporary, fleeting image. The novel clearly exposes the negotiations that go into this subject's construction, specifically Estrella's fragmentation at the crucial moment in the nurse's office: "She felt like two Estrellas. One was a silent phantom who obediently marked a circle with a stick around the bungalow as the mother had requested, while the other held the crowbar and the money" (150). A further fragmentation consists in Estrella's unstable gender boundaries: "Except for the dress she'd pulled over her work clothes, she resembled a young man, standing in the barn's shadow" (74). McCracken points to this nontraditional subject construction when Estrella "rejects the traditional female role by making an unconventional ethical decision" (182). Viramontes here connects to what Sonia Saldívar-Hull describes as a history of Mexican women and Chicanas as mujeres de fuerza (*Feminism* 103–117).

As the barn is not a clearly defined space, it is not a solid platform for Estrella's political action. Viramontes stresses the momentary nature of her protagonist's achievement through various details. First, in the long run, the central social contradictions the novel represents are not resolved. Second, and as a consequence, the family's material conditions have not changed; Perfecto will most likely still leave, Petra has to deal with yet another pregnancy, and she and the children will have to struggle on. Finally, the season is coming to an end and further movement is in store. In this light, the novel's seeming conclusiveness is deceptive and ironic.

Chicana identity, then, as Anzaldúa, Mora, and Viramontes have shown, is in constant process of negotiation and becoming. These Chicanas do not embrace the static selfhood of Humanism, but instead show many similarities to postmodern theories of subjectivity, of fluidity and multiplicity. But in contrast to high postmodernism's somewhat ahistorical conception of subjectivity, Chicanas anchor identity in specific geographic sites and histories. Their characters come of age through negotiating who they are with their physical surroundings such as the South Texas borderlands in Anzaldúa's writings, the marginal spaces in Mora's poetry, and the fields of Southern California in Viramontes's novel. Their characters' biculturalism–being American and Mexican–as well as their ties to a certain place, lead to hybrid identities that are fluid and impermanent, in a constant process of becoming.

Chapter 3

"True Fictions:"
Norma Elía Cantú's Strategic Realism

> White America has a history of examining everybody. You could be a beetle in the rain forest and there'll be a white expert with a camera to photograph you. I think that the white middle class romanticizes the ghetto... White America will only change based on how forceful black people are in our own environment.
>
> Sister Souljah

> Some of us love, and some of us hate, some of us both love and hate our borderlands. Some of us remember, and some of us forget.
>
> Norma Elía Cantú, *Canícula* (132)

At a book signing event, author Amy Tan writes "Truth in Fiction" into my copy of *The Kitchen God's Wife*, her own fictional recreation of China during World War II. Her inscription attests to a recurring concern in contemporary literature with fictional representations of history and a broader examination of the postmodern "crisis of representation" in different fields. This crisis also provides the impetus for Norma Elía Cantú's *Canícula: Snapshots of a Girlhood en la Frontera* (1995), recipient of the Premio Aztlán Literary Prize and second part of a planned trilogy about a family in South Texas and Northern Mexico. In her "Introduction," Cantú characterizes her work as a "fictional autobioethnography." Her self-conscious generic labeling suggests the book's concern with the tensions between fact and fiction, history and literature, ethnography and truth. This concern is furthermore evident when Cantú quotes poet Pat Mora's words: "Life en la Frontera is raw truth, and stories of such life, *fictitious as they may be*, are even truer than true" (xi; emphasis added). Cantú's invocation of Mora's paradoxical statement as well as her passing reference to Roland Barthes's *Camera Lucida: Reflections on Photography*, suggests that what is at stake is the representability of the lives of Mexican Americans in the borderlands.

Canícula dramatizes the tensions between fact and fiction by artfully weaving together the intersecting discourses of autobiography, ethnography, history, and photography, four forms of writing that all traditionally share the assumption of an accurate representability of reality, and that, in the wake of recent poststructuralist theory, have undergone a paradigm shift.[1] This shift accommodates the poststructuralist insight that a reflectionist view of reality ignores that all forms of writing follow certain codes and conventions. In the following, I will analyze these forms of writing from a post-Saussurean (semiotic) perspective. In this view, autobiography, ethnography, historiography, and photography are *languages* whose coded nature problematize direct reflections of reality and draw attention to the medium itself.[2] This view helps highlight Cantú's self-reflexivity in her employment of these languages, which situates her work within postmodern critiques of realism. It echoes current theoretical debates in its dislodging of a one-to-one correspondence between sign and referent. Through many metadiscursive comments, which break the illusion of fiction, Cantú's narrative calls attention to its own linguistic and fictive nature.[3]

Cantú thus participates in a postmodern critique of realist representation while simultaneously and strategically employing realism for didactic purposes.[4] She does so by evoking the discourses of autobiography, ethnography, historiography, and photography for the supposed "certainty" they afford. At the intersection of these discourses Cantú's project emerges: to find a way of representing reality while acknowledging the difficulties of doing so.[5] The urgency to this endeavor arises from the fact that these discourses all carry with them the possibility of the constitution and reconstitution of Mexican American identities. Hers is an important project of resisting dominant autobiographical, ethnographic, historical, and photographic inscriptions, and exposing them as fictions; it is a project of speaking out and talking back.

While a critique of the transparency of the medium is inherent in all, the specificity of each of the four discourses allows for a multi-layered text that enables Cantú to examine this issue from various perspectives. The first discourse, that of autobiography, is always intuitively seen as referential; "autobiography is nothing if not a referential art," says critic Paul John Eakin, author of *Fictions in Autobiography* (quoted in Timothy Dow Adams 463), and as Lorraine M. York points out, the major autobiographical code is to look uncoded (647). However, a one-to-one correspondence to reality is always already questionable: authors retrospectively select, omit, and arrange life materials to achieve a certain effect;

they can gloss over inconsistencies; they can create coherent identities; and they can cover up glitches in the medium that autobiography most relies on: memory. York further explains that in traditional autobiographical theory, this reflectionist view has become the basis for a "humanist universalism," exemplified in James Olney's classic study *Metaphors of the Self.* This view has been challenged by feminist scholars, such as Sidonie Smith, who have shown that traditional autobiography is a gendered, masculinist genre and that women's lives don't fit neatly into existing plot paradigms. As Timothy Dow Adams points out, many female-authored autobiographies display, in effect, a nonlinear and transgressive textuality that challenges notions of referentiality (468).

Canícula recalls traditional autobiographical codes but self-consciously dramatizes their limitations. Cantú does so through a narrative that consists of chronologically fragmented vignettes (85 sections on 132 pages), which collectively create a collage-like portrait of Nena, a young artist. Through fragmentation she stresses the (dis)connections between memory and autobiography in the process of constructing identity. Cantú focuses on the retrospective reshaping of one's life by warning readers up front that "what may appear to be autobiographical is not always so" (xi). She further counters the universalism and individualism inherent in traditional autobiographies by depicting Nena as a bicultural individual, juggling two cultures, two languages, and two histories, as a person deeply embedded in a community context.

Second, Cantú's generic hybridization experimentally links the autobiographical story of the self to the ethnographic story of Nena's social and cultural environment.[6] Until the 1960s ethnography had commonly been regarded as an "objective" science. Ethnographers are, in this view, mere recorders of experiences and cultural encounters. In his "Introduction" to *Writing Culture: The Poetics and Politics of Ethnography,* James Clifford takes on the persistent ideology of the transparency of ethnographic representation and argues that "literary processes . . . affect the ways cultural phenomena are registered" (4). Clifford places his approach within current postmodern and poststructuralist positions, according to which "what appears as 'real' . . . is always analyzable as a restrictive and expressive set of social codes and conventions" (10). Ethnographic writing, he continues, "is an 'art,' . . . the skillful fashioning of useful artifacts" (6). The boundaries, then, between ethnography and fiction, as the ones between autobiography and fiction, begin to blur.[7] Moreover, this critique includes a challenge to the "objectivity" of ethnographers, who frequently become the main characters in their fiction and oftentimes disguise their power. The essays that follow Clifford's introduction testify to this "crisis" in ethnography, the current tendency to dislodge secure representation.[8] Cantú's use of the term "ethnography" signals an awareness of an Anglo-American audience and of previous ethnographic writings about Mexican Americans. She presents a postmodern counter-ethnography that revises dominant culture's stories about Mexican Americans and depicts Nena and her people as active participants in and questioning subjects of both cultures' epistemologies. *Canícula* further presents a panoramic view of life in the borderlands and, as we will see, functions as an allegory of the loss of traditions.

Thirdly, though "history" is not part of Cantú' s generic label, it nonetheless figures prominently as a narrative subtext. The work captures the Mexican American community from the Great Depression into the 1950s, and Nena describes the effects of changing immigration policies and social and ethnic relations in the borderlands during that time. Cantú offers a revisionist history, a history that is constructed through a multitude of private stories situated at the crossroads of official history and politics. Her strategy builds on New Historicist discourses, which have challenged traditional historiography's stance of neutrality and objectivity. Like autobiographers and ethnographers, historians select and arrange their materials for presentation since only through their arrangement do data and facts become meaningful. As Trachtenberg explains, "Facts must be made legible and intelligible, must be given an order and a meaning which does not crush their autonomy as facts" (xiv). Hayden White has been instrumental in showing the narrative, and even literary arrangement, of history writing. In "The Historical Text as Literary Artifact," he lists a series of questions a "meta-history" must explore:

> What is the structure of a peculiarly *historical* consciousness? What is the epistemological status of historical explanations, as compared with other kinds of explanations that might be offered to account for the materials with which historians ordinarily deal? What are possible forms of historical representation and what are their bases? What authority can historical accounts claim as contributions to a secured knowledge of reality in general and to the human sciences in particular? (81)

White opens up inquiry into how such arrangement might impinge on historical accuracy and concludes his call for a meta-history with the words,

> . . . in general there has been a reluctance to consider historical narratives as what they most manifestly are: verbal fictions, the contents of which are as much invented as found and the forms of which have more in common with their counterparts in literature than they have with those in the sciences. (90)[9]

More recently Leticia Garza Falcon has chosen the case of Walter Prescott Webb, whose seminal work *The Texas Rangers* (1935) has for decades governed discussions of race and ethnicity in Texas. In New Historicist fashion, Garza-Falcon exposes this book as a racist fiction disguised as history.

Fourthly, in her "Introduction" Cantú places special importance on photography: "In *Canícula*," she writes, "the story is told through the photographs" (xi). Photography is the discourse that most vividly dramatizes the tensions between fact and fiction. But if photography is the dominant code in the narrative, it governs not just a reading of the images but of the surrounding text as well. In other words, the autobiographical, ethnographic, and historical narratives are created through and surrounded by photography. The snapshots, twenty-three photographs recording Nena's growth, her family, and her environment, are interspersed in the short narrative sections, *briccoleur*-style. These photographs form a text that interrogates the (dis)connections between the pictures and the stories, between the verbal and the visual, raising epistemological questions of realism, truth, and the representability of Mexican American experiences in the traditional novel form, questions that are common to much of postmodern literature and theory.

Like Cantú's literary predecessor, Ishmael Reed, who created a fictional history of African Americans in his novel *Mumbo Jumbo*, *Canícula* creates a panoramic view of life on the border. As in *Mumbo Jumbo*, the photographs in this book serve as authentication devices, providing ontological certainty. French critic Roland Barthes, referred to in Cantú's introduction, and transformed in her book into a fictional character whose death in 1980 coincides with two lovers in Madrid sorting through a box of pictures, ponders the essential nature of the photograph in *Camera Lucida: Reflections on Photography*. He argues that the photograph's defining quality lies in its tie to an external referent (5): "The very essence, the *noeme* of Photography," he writes, is the reality of the past: "In Photography I can never deny that *the thing has been there*" (76–7). Hence photography, unlike writing, quite unequivocally offers "experiential order of proof" (79). Barthes argues against supporters of semantic relativism who believe in the coded nature of photographs and instead proclaims himself to be a realist who does not "take the photograph for a 'copy' of reality, but for an emanation of *past reality*, a *magic*, not an art" (88). He concludes, "From a phenomenological viewpoint, in the Photograph, the power of authentication exceeds the power of representation" (89).[10]

While Barthes denies links between photography and other art forms, postmodern critics focus precisely on those connections because they detract from the certainty of the photograph. American cultural critic Susan Sontag and British art historian John Berger discuss photography within a larger socio-economic and cultural context and warn against confusing photographs with "utter truth." Both focus on photography as a form of representation with multiple meanings attached to it. Berger explains that the nature of the appearances the camera transports are both constructed *and* natural. While the image may be an immediate and unconstructed quotation from reality, the photographer's choice is a matter of cultural construction, presenting *his* reading of events. As Trachtenberg argues for history, as an isolated fact, or quotation, the photograph is disconnected from continuity and does not in itself constitute meaning. Photographs are meaningful only when they are embedded in a context. Berger's comments suggest that the common-sense idea of the truthfulness of pictures must be challenged.

Sontag more clearly relates photography to other art forms. While also acknowledging that photography serves as a quotation from the past that may seem more authentic than fiction (74), she nonetheless sees it as much of an interpretation of the world as are paintings and writing. In her view, photography is a "composition," subject to the selective choices of the photographers, the tastes of a culture, and the rules of genres (nude photography, portrait photography), which all participate in the creation of meaning (105–6). Like Berger, Sontag places great emphasis on context:

> Because each photograph is a fragment, its moral and emotional weight depends on where it is inserted. A photograph changes according to the context in which it is seen . . . As Wittgenstein argued for words, that the meaning *is* the use—so for each photograph. And it is in this way that the presence and proliferation of all photographs contributes to the erosion of the very notion of meaning, to that parceling out of the truth into relative truths. (105–6)

Photographic meaning hence is never stable.

Recent publications have more radically argued for the instability of meaning and photography's inherent impulse to deconstruct reality. In his book, *Burning with Desire: The Conception of Photography*, Geoffrey Batchen suggests that the rise of photography coincided with a period of radical rethinking of reality and representation. He argues that from its inception, photography was not devoted to capturing reality but to deconstructing it. His most prominent example, also evoked by Michael Sapir in his essay "The Impossible Photograph," is how

Hippolyte Bayard, the inventor of photography, challenges photographic positivism in his series of self-portraits as a drowned man, complete with suicide note on the back of the image. Moreover, both Sapir and John Tagg, in his *The Burden of Representation: Essays on Photographies and Histories*, show that photographic procedure is a direct reflection of contemporary thinking. Specifically, it is modeled on contemporary views of space and a chemical process where reactions depend on the composition and density of the paper, which allows for different versions of reality—all contradictory to what Trachtenberg calls the "myth of the unerring objective camera" (19). Tagg concludes by countering Barthes's assumptions, "The photograph is not a magical 'emanation' but a material product of a material apparatus set to work in specific contexts, by specific forces, for more or less defined purposes" (3).

In the vein of a Foucauldian archaeology of knowledge, both Tagg and Sontag further question photography's connections to realist representation by showing the constructed nature of the link between photography and "evidence." Both explain photography as a function of the state, which, in the nineteenth century, formed institutions and practices of record-keeping, including criminology, anthropological sciences, and natural sciences that centered around the body and its environment. Tagg argues that photographic documentation and evidence came into existence within the context of a historical shift in power. The real issue, he concludes, is not realism but power, the power of representation—certainly an important concern for Mexican American writers as well.

Like Reed, Cantú strategically uses the discourse of authenticity surrounding photography to confer authority on the version of history *Canícula* offers. Many of her images are, as the title announces, snapshots, and snapshots in particular are a genre that does not seem bounded by photographic conventions. In Tessa DeCarlo's analysis, they stand out through their "artless style and family-record function" (3), and according to San Francisco photographer Linda Connor, "They have a spontaneity, a veracity that can be considered naive and unsophisticated" (De Carlo 3). Connor further calls snapshots a version of "vernacular photography," that is, one of "the many varieties of photography made without art in mind" (30).[11] But snapshots can also be seen as constituting a kind of documentary photography imitated and then appropriated by professional photographers, an effect that is enhanced by the black and white nature of the images in the book.

Like the short reflective sections in Barthes's *Camera Lucida*, Cantú's narrative practices mirror the process of piecing together photographs; the text, as Cantú explains in the "Introduction," "does not adhere to conventions of plot development. Instead it is a collage of stories gleaned from photographs randomly picked, not from a photo album chronologically arranged, but haphazardly pulled from a box of photos where time is blurred" (xii). Cantú's chronologically fragmented vignettes—doubly framed through the "Introduction" and the third-person "Preface"—are like snapshots themselves, short, descriptive, and crystallizing a character or an event. Like photos, they appear to be disconnected and autonomous units, but collectively, they compile Nena's life story. Nena, the narrator of most sections, thinks of herself as a camera, "freezing images in time" (37), with the same desire to record and to inventory her world (Sontag 37). Typically, the photograph will serve as the kernel, the occasion, the situation, around which the narrative revolves. Like a life-fostering growth, it creates narrative. But the term "kernel" also captures the static nature of the photograph, its "thereness," truth-value, unrepeatability, and arrest of time. The narrative then functions as a supplement to the photos, elaborating, contextualizing, providing information and facts for the reader. As Berger shows, the photograph's static nature is, when embedded in text, counteracted by the narrative's flow, encompassing past, present, and future, and creating context and historicity (89). Together, the photos and the text become "undefeatable."

Ostensibly, then, Cantú's narrative supports Barthes's photographic realism. Like the correspondence and documents that compose the first part of the trilogy, in this narrative photographs serve as a tool for asserting certitude. This certitude, however, she immediately undermines. The relation between photography and narrative provides ample potential for an ironic juxtaposition of fact and fiction. The narrator explains, "for some of these events there are photographs; for others, the image is a collage; and in all cases, the result is entirely of my doing." She continues, "So although it may appear that these stories are my family's, they are not precisely, and yet they are" (xi). Statements such as this one give rise to several questions. First, and most fundamentally, who is Nena? Is she identical in the successive pictures with the author? Is "Nena" then a thinly disguised persona for the author? But Cantú reminds us "In *Canícula* the story is told through the photographs, and so what may appear to be autobiographical is not always so. On the other hand, many of the events are completely fictional, although they may be true in a historical context" (xi).

Second, as I have suggested, it is through the text that the images take on meaning for the reader. Typically, the sections begin with descriptions of the picture, of its location, time, and characters. As a narrative mode, description is closely tied to realism, especially when we can "verify" the portrait by comparing text and image. However, Nena does not merely record but also interprets, compares, and explains. For Nena, as for Barthes when he is looking at photographs of his mother, what is in the foreground is the subjective and personal truths the images contain. For instance, she recalls when looking at a picture of a parade which she attends perched on her father's shoulders: "So comforting, so secure to be held aloft and feel the security, the strength of his arms. So many times he held me" (37). Moreover, Nena, as an artist in the making, not only presents herself as a recorder of events but as a storyteller as well, one who makes others' stories her own, "embellishing to fit my plots" (9), a statement which complicates the reality-status of her creations.

Though we cannot verify them, the photographs tease us into believing the memories related in the narrative sections. Frequently memories lead to tellings of what is both spatially and temporally *outside* of the picture's frame. For instance, the picture that heads the section "Rocking Horse" presents "Nena" as a three-year-old, sitting unsmiling on a toy horse. Like others, this vignette begins with a verbal transcription of the image: "My feet sandaled in brown huaraches from Nuevo Laredo with tiny nopales and tinier red pears . . ." (6), but it then traverses the frame of the picture: "I look straight at the camera at mami who's kneeling on one knee to be at eye level with me" (6). Similarly, the picture that heads the "May" section, portraying "Nena," her younger sister, brother, and Bueli, begins with a description of the location and then of the fine clothes the family is wearing. But the fourth sentence, beginning with "Later we'll pick flowers . . ." (4), already gives rise to more general reflections, which govern the rest of the vignette. In Proustian fashion, then, Nena recalls her childhood through the scent of the particular flowers and the taste of the candy the children will receive. And the words, as Berger explains in a different context, are given authenticity by the irrefutablity of photography (92).

Third, the narrator dramatizes her own power of selection, of inclusion or exclusion, for reasons undisclosed to the reader, by, more often than not, describing photographs from memory *without* reprinting them. To develop this "prose picture" or "imagetext," as Marianne Hirsch calls it (9), Cantú uses photographic language, present tense narration, an accumulation of descriptive detail, and list-like representation of "characters." The section "Last Piñata," for instance, follows the pattern set up earlier. It begins by announcing the location and continues by describing the imaginary picture: "We're in our backyard for my last birthday piñata. In the foreground the piñata in the shape of a birthday cake. . ." (54). Or the section "Papi's Horse" begins with "My father is on his favorite horse. He wears a hat that casts a shadow over his face, but I can tell he's smiling his 'I'm-so-proud-smile.' He's young in the photo . . ." (15). Based on previous viewing and reading, the reader is teased into trusting the narrator's descriptions and creates a mental image of the photograph.

Fourth, and most importantly, the narrator dramatizes disconnections between memory and reality through occasional discrepancies between image and narrative description. For instance, the "Bueli" vignette is preceded by a picture of Bueli with three girls, but the narrator claims that she herself *and* three siblings are in the picture. Similarly, the "Tino" vignette is headed by a photograph with the inscription "Easter 1952" that depicts four children in the backyard. The focus is on Tino, Nena's brother: "He stands to the side with his hand out as if pointing a gun or a rifle," a posture recognizable in the picture to the reader. However, the narrator continues, "Everyone else is crowded around me; the piñata in the shape of a birthday cake sways in the wind above our heads" (14). Clearly, the description does not coincide with the image and may rather refer to a mental image or a conflation of photographs in Nena's mind. Moreover, the narrative proclaims "ten years later, 1968, he is a soldier, and it's not a game. And we are gathered again," this time for Tino's funeral (14). If the inscription is correct, ten years later would be 1962, not 1968. Inconsistencies such as these point to the precarious process of reconstructing events from memory. As Sontag reminds us, what we remember is a truth but not necessarily *the* truth; seeing and remembering is always subjective (Sontag 136).

Fifth, the relation between photographs and reality is furthermore revealed as tenuous when the narrative points out what the photos conceal. Snapshots that function as souvenirs from the past tend to cover up contradictions and focus on joyous occasions. For instance, "Las Piscas" describes a picture—not reprinted in the text—of the family picking cotton, and the image gives rise in the narrator's mind to memories of being in the fields. She comments, "In the photo, smiles belie tired, aching feet and backs; smiles on serious faces, stiff bodies posed for life" (3), a picture that reminds me of FSA photographs of migrant workers, about which more later. At times, what is concealed is more important than what is revealed.

Cantú's strategy consists of drawing on the photographs' irrefutability to validate the story but also to confer importance on Mexican American experiences, especially as they are reprinted and circulated in book-form.[12] Through its interaction with the text, the photograph ceases to be the de-contextualized art Paul de Man envisions, but instead helps tell three stories:[13] the autobiographical story of Nena's personal growth, the ethnographic story of borderland culture, and the historical story of Mexican Americans in South Texas. First, the autobiographical story of *Canícula* is the story of the bicultural individual who shapes her past through her memories. The images that head or interrupt the narrative sections are family pictures, recording Nena's growth as well as important family events, including births, deaths, gatherings, and trips, thus clearly embedding Nena in a social context. In the amateur snapshots Nena finds as she rifles through the box of pictures, people appear in their own, everyday environment: for example Bueli with the kids outside the house, and Nena in her blue stroller or on the rocking horse. In the photographs, she discovers the history of her childhood. Apart from amateur snapshots, she also finds pictures taken by professional photographers. Professional family photography, in Pierre Bourdieu's view, has a social function, of "solemnizing and immortalizing the high points in family life—reinforcing the integration of the family group" (19). For Bourdieu, the family album is the essence of social memory (30).[14] Nena's family album clearly function this way: Here we find Nena's first birthday picture, school pictures, wedding pictures of the family, and Nena's first communion picture. Jokingly, the narrative explains that due to a mix-up Nena actually had two first communions. This admission shows Cantú's ironic play with the function of photography to solemnize momentous occasions in individual and family lives by raising the question of whether the reprinted image is the "correct" one.

While some of the photographs stress the child's embeddedness in a family context, others foreground Nena's ideological identity formation, most prominently revolving around the issue of her citizenship. To do so, Cantú reprints two documents, both U.S. immigration papers, showing pictures of Nena as a baby and at age twelve, and declaring her Mexican nationality. Like many teenagers, she struggles with the question "Who am I?" (21), but unlike European American teenagers, this issue is exacerbated due to her status as a hyphenated individual. As a girl who has grown up this side of the border, she is confused at being "declared a Mexican national" (21). This imposed identity leaves her unsettled since she feels like an outsider in Mexico and clearly identifies with the United States. Thus, when in Mexico, she is "homesick for my U.S. world full of TV . . . I'm homesick and I don't have a [Spanish] word for it" (22–23). She compares her own confrontation with borders with her Mother's carefree youth; she had "family on both sides of a river that's never a barrier; after all, she's Texas-born, her land lies beyond borders" (42). While Nena is more at home in the U.S., she repeatedly witnesses and is impressed by the older generation's pride in their Mexican heritage: at the parade celebrating George Washington's birthday in her hometown Laredo, she reports that "when the flags go by, the men take off their hats, and everyone places a hand over their heart—the same for the U.S. or the Mexican flag, but when the Mexican flag goes by someone in the crowd shouts, '¡Viva México!' and everyone answers '¡Viva!'" (37). As José Limón explains, this parade was institutionalized in Laredo in 1897 to assimilate Mexican Americans into the American mainstream (*Dancing* 41). The older generation's subversive reaction here instructs Nena about what is at stake in her ideological identity formation.

That identity formation is a constant process of oscillation between different cultural voices, codes, or ideologies, as Mikhail Bakhtin points out.[15] Like many Mexican American teenagers, she internalizes U.S. American cultural codes due to the impact of socialization agencies such as educational and cultural institutions. During her adolescence, Nena tries hard to assimilate to the dominant system; she and her friends listen to mostly English music, and aspects of her Mexican heritage seem "too Spanish" to her. When watching Western movies, she marvels at the depiction of cowboys fighting Indians, so different from Mexican TV. As children, Nena and her friends would imitate these movie plots; her first story even derives from such a plot (34). While early on the impact of mass-disseminated images and myths is stronger than life experiences, the older retrospective narrator demystifies norms and expectations disseminated in popular culture and comments, "And all the while, my uncles in Anáhuac herding cattle and being real cowboys, my aunts living out stories no fifties scriptwriter . . . ever divined" (34).

As we have seen above, "family photography is both an index and an instrument of [social] integration" (Bourdieu 40). But because of this, Berger explains, photographs are "more traumatic than most memories because they seem to confirm, prophetically, the later discontinuity created by absence or death" (87). Sontag's epigraph to *Canícula*, "All photographs are *memento mori*" sets up a theme that runs through the narrative.[16] The Easter 1952 picture is a case in point. Nena reads Tino's pose as a foreshadowing of his future occupation and cause of his death; surrounded by the other children, he stands "as if pointing a gun or a rifle"

(14). This image and narration points out several things about the interaction between memory and photography. First, it shows the contiguous/metonymic ways in which memory works: "He did it at four. And again at nine" (14). "And he's playing, even in the picture, at being a soldier. Only ten years later, 1968, he is a soldier, and it's not a game" (14). To emphasize Tino's social role as a soldier, she includes an image of her brother in uniform. Similarly, when looking at the picture of Bueli in her room with the kids, the photograph reminds her of a *later* instance, the time of her death, when "In the very same room, we prayed around her coffin" (24). Secondly, it attests to a habit of retrospectively reading the fate of a person into the photograph, even if the picture is taken at a much earlier point. This retrospective foreshadowing or looking into the future of the past, becomes a habit when Nena sorts through her family's pictures. Many sections thus recount losses and betray her concern with time, a larger thematic desire to arrest time, as does the photograph.

While these mostly private pictures outline Nena's maturation, they simultaneously tell a larger story: an ethnographic narrative of borderland cultures, signaled at the beginning of the book through an area map that depicts the geographical space of South Texas and Northern Mexico. This map places the narrative within ethnographic traditions and ironically signals the narrator's exploration of this little-known part of the world, South Texas, which constituted for early ethnographers, as Jose Davíd Saldívar suggests, "the American heart of darkness" (*Border Matters* 164).[17] Through the ethnographic narrative Cantú provides a panoramic view of borderlands society and exposes power relations. It further enables her to present a collective *memento mori* for the loss of Mexican American culture.

In *Camera Lucida* Barthes points to photography's ethnographic function, which is to relay *information*: "Since the photograph is pure contingency and can be nothing else (it is always *something* that is represented)—contrary to the text which, by the sudden action of a single word, can shift a sentence from description to reflection—it immediately yields up those 'details' which constituted the very raw material of ethnological knowledge" (28). As we have seen, the link between photography and meaning is more complicated than Barthes has made it out to be. While Tagg agrees with Barthes that photography can serve as a form of visual anthropology, he clearly points out the potential power relations involved. Since the nineteenth century, he argues, colonized peoples were subjected to the "scrutinizing gaze" and "rendered incapable of speaking, acting, or organizing for themselves" (11). Similarly Sidonie Smith has suggested that photography in the postcolonial contact zone frequently becomes an apparatus of colonialism, used by colonial institutions. "Photos," she argues, "became one means through which the formerly unknown, profoundly different and exotic other, could be catalogued, captioned, and domesticated within the frames of the colonizer's lens" (527).

Indeed, Cantú's pictorial narrative forms, in part, a response to the images of Mexicans commissioned by the FSA (Farm Security Association) in the 1930s and 40s. Collected in *Picturing Texas: The FSA-OWI Photographers in the Lone Star State 1935–1943,* these images dramatize the plight of the poor and depict them at home and at work—in the cotton fields, the carrot fields, the pecan shelleries. Like all FSA-commissioned images, the photos are powerful documents of rural poverty, helplessness, and insufficiency, where sickness is a common motif. They also show people deeply implicated in a politics of domination and dependency. For example, one image shows a worker in a static pose suggestive of the photographer's presence, in the carrot fields, proudly showing the results of his labor. The photographs frequently draw attention to the people's foreignness. The caption to one of Russell Lee's images reads: "Children of Mexican labor contractor in their home. Note the shrine above the children. Shrines like the one above the children are found in practically all Mexican homes" (34). Captions such as this one point to the ethnographic project in the series and frequently depict Mexicans as exotic objects. Another example is Lee's photo of a Mexican housewife standing in a curtain made of bottle caps (164). Noteworthy is further his series "San Antonio, Mexican Section," and particularly "Mexican Woman in Her Home," where the woman's upper body and head are in the lower fourth of the picture, while the rest of the image depicts the newspaper wallpaper, clothes hanging on the left, calendars, and family pictures on the wall, providing an inventory of her surroundings as recognizably "Mexican." One of the most compelling and, according to Robert Reed, best known FSA images is Dorothea Lange's "Migrant Mother"—the gaunt, haggard, unsmiling portrait of a Mexican (Indian) woman. Despite the project's reformist intentions, and despite the supposedly mimetic representations, the overall effect these images create is one of the Otherness of Mexican Americans, who appear like static museum exhibits. None of the workers is identified as an American citizen, and the images thus reify their difference.[18]

I intend to read Cantú's images as responses to these state-commissioned images capturing the lives of "Mexicans." As we have seen, one of the main ideas foregrounded in the autobiographical story is Nena's *Mexican Americanness* and her feelings of allegiance to this country, complicating her ethnicity and showing her in a web of relations to both nations. Her identity is not monological. While the FSA pictures are public images with artistic aspirations, when the camera is in the hands of the ethnographic subject, a different story emerges. This story does not depict its subjects as static and in isolation, but within a broader social and family context. Rather than stressing difference, the reprinted images invite readers' identification with the characters, not distance and detachment from them. Thus Cantú's project can be seen as a form of resistance, of talking back, of assembling her own cultural collage.

While clearly the photographic collage on the cover of the book draws attention to itself and the fabricated nature of photographic impression, it also functions as an ideogram, suggesting symbols or icons of both Mexcian and American cultures. It is made up of images and objects that suggest an entire context of what it means to grow up Mexican American. It includes a passport, a rosary, the narrator's first communion picture, her siblings, her mother, her grandmother, images of Jesus—all laid on top of a white Christening gown embroidered with hearts and with the image of a white girl praying. Taken together, the images in the book form a collage that provide readers with *information*, with ethnographic knowledge of what it means to live on the border (Barthes). The story the photographs tell concerns larger cultural truths—of the importance, for instance, of first communion.

The narrative vignettes clearly break up Nena's monologic voice as well as constructions of a monologic identity through various devices. First, through repeated digressions Nena includes a multitude of stories, oftentimes only tangentially related to her growth. In dialogic and polyphonic fashion Cantú depicts a web of family relations—comadres and compadres, friends and neighbors—to represent the diversity within the Mexican American community. "The family," Nena reflects, "extending sideways uncles, aunts, cousins; and back into the past parents, grandparents, great-grandparents; and toward children, grandchildren, to today. The Bodas de Oro—golden anniversary celebrating survival, celebrating endurance, celebrating family" (83). There is the story, for instance, of Mamagrande, born into Mexican nobility but impoverished after her marriage and move to the U.S.; the story of cousin Elisa, sent away after being seduced, who is now enslaved to her Chicano husband; the story of Mamagrande's cousin's daughter who used to be a free-spirited teenager and becomes a solemn, quiet woman, only concerned with her children in Iran; the story of Nena's friend's rape; or school friend Sanjuana's story of quitting school and taking care of her siblings. But there are also narratives that contradict the image of Mexican Americans as victims of domination, including sister Dahlia's story of self-assertion, when she gets a job so far reserved only for boys, or stories about the female support system of the comadres—a celebration of mujeres.

The interaction of photo and text further destabilizes dominant images of Mexican Americans and, more importantly, of "ethnic identity" itself. For example, one image depicts Nena's mother in the china poblana, a traditional Mexican costume. The photo is taken on a main town square in Nuevo Laredo and functions as a ritualized symbol of her mexicanidad. It is a typical ideogram (Bourdieu), the text's only example of radical, essentialized Otherness (Fusco). However, this section is part of a china poblana picture series and is preceded by a vignette entitled "China Poblana One," depicting Nena in a version of the same costume, but creating a distinct contrast between the two. Whereas the mother's picture is a symbolic ideogram of Mexican traditional identity—complete with Mexican hat, colorfully embroidered shirt and wide skirt depicting an eagle—Nena poses in a more private place, outside the family house, and her attire only marginally resembles the official costume. These versions of the same motif show that ethnic identity is not static but constantly in the process of (re)definition.

Challenging traditional ethnographic depictions of Mexican Americans may be one goal of the book: another most certainly is inscribing Mexican American culture for posterity through the creation of a collective *memento mori*. The various stories embedded in Nena's life story collectively present the rich legacy of Mexican American culture in the borderlands. While Nena's descriptions provide personal and communal narratives of day-to-day life, including natural and political catastrophes such as floods and deportations, major and minor personal events such as births, deaths, and bee stings, they also focus to a large extent on culture and include reference to remedios, fiestas, religion, cooking, folklore, holidays, cultural change, poverty, dichos, Christmas traditions, and languages. Cantú characteristically uses iterative descriptions when discussing holidays such as Christmas or the Day of the Dead, conscious of her non-Mexican American audience. According to Octavio Paz, the Mexican love of fiestas and public gatherings serves like Sontag's photography, to "stop the flow of time and commemorate men and events" (49). He claims, "the day is a pause: time is stopped; it is actually annihilated" (50).

If ethnography is largely allegorical, as Clifford claims, Cantú's allegory revolves around the infiltration of U.S. popular culture into Mexican American society and a consequent gradual loss of Mexican traditions. For example, Cantú dedicates five narrative sections to the celebration of the Day of the Dead. Nena remembers the ritual of going to the cemetery and telling the stories of the deceased: the story of cousin Raúl, who goes crazy from too much reading, or the story of Lucíta, whose death was foretold by a gypsy. When Nena returns thirty years later, she sees changes everywhere; symbols of Halloween have replaced Mexican customs. Her narrative, then, becomes simultaneously a repository of cultural memory.

As the narrative counters traditional ethnographic depictions of Mexican Americans, it also resists official histories that have presented the history of South Texas as one of conquest and domination. In his *Anglos and Mexicans in the Making of Texas, 1836–1986*, David Montejano argues that the history of this area is endowed with a "culture of race-thinking" (159). Within the context of the U.S.'s attempts at nation-building, Mexican Americans have been described as un-American and unassimilable. As an exponent of this thinking Walter Prescott Webb comes to mind, whose portrayals of Mexican Americans have long been taken as historical fact. Generalizations such as the following are common in his work:

> Without disparagement, it may be said that there is a cruel streak in the Mexican nature, or so the history of Texas would lead one to believe. This cruelty may be a heritage from the Spanish of the Inquisition; it may, and doubtless should, be attributed partly to the Indian blood. . . . The Mexican warrior . . . on the whole, is inferior to the Comanche and wholly unequal to the Texan. (Webb 14; quoted in Garza-Falcón 1)

Webb's use of the binary opposition of Texan and Mexican is indicative of a sense of racial superiority and affirmed beliefs of the settlers as "white folks" (Montejano 29). Leticia Garza-Falcón offers a rigorous critique of Webb's position and shows how the eminent University of Texas historian "legitimize[d] as 'proper' history a story already in construction" (1). This story is shaped by a variety of literary devices and a paradigm that Webb had already developed in *The Great Plains*: of great frontiersmen succeeding against the odds due to their rugged individualism. *The Texas Rangers* presents another version of this romance quest, but frontiersmen are replaced by the rangers who fight and win against the undesirable Mexican element.[19]

To this official history, Cantú adds Nena's personal story, one that is aware of its own historical construction, as the time frame announced in the Introduction indicates. It foregrounds rather than mystifies the idea of history as narrative and presents itself as individual and cultural counter-memory. Historical events, most importantly the Great Depression, deportations, and the Bracero program of the 1940s and 50s, are filtered here through personal memories and captured in both words and pictures. Gloria Anzaldúa's epigraph on the border points to the precarious political situation many Mexican Americans find themselves in; words like "open wound," "grates," and "bleeds" create a sense of violence and transgression. And the narrative takes up a particularly painful moment in recent history: the expulsion of Mexican Americans from their homeland. Looking at a picture of the family crossing the border to the U.S. in 1948, Bueli tells Nena the story how in 1935 she and her Texas-born grandfather were forced to undertake the reverse journey:

> [They] drove their pickup truck down from San Antonio. They felt lucky; most deportees left with nothing but the clothes on their back, sent in packed trains to the border on the way to Mexico, even those who were U.S. citizens. She told of crossing from one Laredo to the other and losing everything—Buelito's pride and joy, a black Ford pickup truck and all their belongings—to the corrupt customs officials at the border. (5)

One photograph shows Nena's maternal grandfather, "his right foot on one end of the running board of the Ford and a teddy bear on the other end." Looking at the picture, her aunt recalls—and relives—the experience of deportation the photo does not hint at:

> How Papá loved his car! . . . He was so proud of his truck, too. I think that's what hurt him most when we left San Antonio; he sold the green car and bought a black pickup truck so we could bring all our furniture, everything back to Mexico. I don't think he minded losing everything as much as he minded losing the truck. (110)

In 1948 then, the south-north crossing "meant coming home, but not quite" (50). Existence in the U.S. is still tenuous; el norte is both home and a foreign country. By focusing on her family's experience of deportation, Nena connects her story with the political history of Mexican Americans in the U.S.

Looking back at my epigraph about loving and hating the borderlands, it becomes clear that the act of remembering and recording, through both photographs and narrative, becomes an act of love, an act of preservation and recovery. The point is not to certify Nena's versions as historical truth; instead the protagonist becomes synecdochal figure for larger cultural, political, and historical realities in South Texas. Mora's paradoxical statement about life *en la frontera* as raw truth suggests what is at stake here: not of capturing historical truth of an individual's life, not certifying Nena's life story, but the larger historical truth of a collective of which the individual is a representative, and which does not have to depend upon factual accuracy. Nena's life is the nexus of extended family, and of the cultural, political, and historical realities of life in South Texas. As in much postmodern literature, truth is represented through fiction.

Chapter 4

Little Women Meets *The Flintstones*: Mixing Genres and Blending Cultures in Ana Castillo's *So Far From God* and Sandra Cisneros's "Little Miracles, Kept Promises"

We possess nothing; rather, we are inhabitants of a world of fictions, a world constructed by our need for meaning, for stability, for possession. The meanings we believe grounded in some essential reality are seen to be mere projections of our desire and hope. Every human act and statement creates a world and establishes a context of value. But these acts are ultimately meaningless. Their significance lies only in the patterns of desire and belief, or of assertion and doubt, that they reveal. So that once one is free of the delusions of essential meaning, free to perceive and self-consciously participate in the free play of the creation and necessary denial of meaning, one may rejoice, as does [John] Cage, in unrestricted creativity.

Charles Russell, *The Avant-Garde Today* (101)

In his reading of Maurice Blanchot's *La Folie du jour* [Madness of Day], Jacques Derrida argues for the impossibility of adhering to categorical delineations of genre. "The Law of Genre," in his view, is a prescriptive, "authoritarian summons to a law of a 'do' or 'do not'" (56). This summons is followed by rules and interdictions: "One must respect a norm, one must not cross a line of demarcation, one must not risk impurity, anomaly, or monstrosity" (57). Further, genres should not intermix, since purity is "the law of the law of genre" (57). It is precisely this law that Derrida interrogates: "What if there were, lodged within the heart of the law itself, a law of impurity or a principle of contamination? And suppose the condition for the possibility of the law were the *a priori* of a counterlaw, an axiom of impossibility that would confound its sense, order, and reason?" (57). The latter quote gets at the crux of Derrida's poststructuralist endeavor: to challenge

Enlightenment principles that sought to establish "sense, order, and reason" as the apex of human achievement. As his rhetoric demonstrates, these normative values were underscored by legalistic/punitive measures.

Blanchot's text, then, which self-reflexively focuses on the narrator's inability to give a coherent account (*récit*) of the events that occurred to him, announces itself as a specific type of narrative (*récit*) that puts its own narrative demarcations to the test, and that does, in fact, question narratability itself. The text is recursive, nonlinear, plotless, and does not provide the "sense" the listeners/readers expect from the narrator. In Derrida's representation, Blanchot's text "makes light of all the tranquil categories of genre-theory and history in order to upset their taxonomic certainties . . . the presumed stability of their classical nomenclatures" (63).[1] The "taxonomic certainties" genre theories like to project, and which Blanchot questions, include "the value of an event, first of all, of reality, of fiction, of appearance, and so on" (68). As Derrida, using the "exemplary" text by Blanchot, challenges the law, he simultaneously points out the ludic nature of Blanchot's enterprise—his play with the conventions of narrative and of reading—as well as of the poststructuralist transgressive project in general that replaces law with play: "What *game* is the law, a law of this genre, *playing*? . . . *La Folie du jour plays* down the law, *plays* at the law, *plays* with the law" (79; emphasis added).

The idea that freedom from the law allows for free play and subversion of meaning has become a staple of high postmodern discourses. Thus Charles Russell calls the statements in the above epigraph, taken from the beginning of his chapter "Towards an Aesthetics of Play and Disruption", "a declaration of postmodernist faith, . . . the basis of most recent experimental and avant-garde art" (101). And a number of well-known postmodern artists have explored the creative possibilities through defying the law of genre. John Barth's title story in his collection *Lost in the Funhouse* (1968) perhaps most strikingly questions the narrative conventions deriving from nineteenth-century realistic fiction and, like *La Folie du jour*, interrogates the nature and possibility of storytelling itself. Barth here features storytelling that interrupts itself for frequent metanarrative comments, establishing the notion that fictional conventions simultaneously shape and mask reality. Such metanarrative comments include ruminations on the nature of language, realism, authorship, and romance. What distinguishes postmodern writers from their predecessors is an inherent reflexivity on the fiction-making activity.

Certainly disruption and play are at work in Barth's skewering of generic conventions, as they are in the writing of many Chicanas. But the repeated emphasis in postmodern discourses on the meaninglessness of such manipulation is clearly questioned in Chicana texts. Linda Hutcheon's formulations are always helpful in defining and refining this aspect of postmodern fiction. She characterizes postmodern texts' relation with past forms of representation as a simultaneous "use and abuse of conventions" and argues that there is "a contradictory dependence on and independence from that which temporally preceded it"; postmodern fiction is a critical and parodic revisitation and "repetition with critical distance that allows ironic signaling of difference at the very heart of similarity" (*Poetics* 18; 26). Rather than a focus on the play of signifier, Hutcheon provides a pathway towards an understanding of generic disruption as engagement with the social and political. The purpose is to expose the old structures and their production of meaning and to replace them with new forms. Postmodern writers use older forms critically to reveal how they construct reality and how that reality is ideologically determined.

Both Marxist and feminist critics have noted that generic conventions are mechanisms of social control and foreground the links between aesthetics and politics. Fredric Jameson, for example, has called narrative a "socially symbolic act" that functions as a "social contract" (*Political Unconscious* 20; 106). Jameson insists that genre and mode are conventions that constrain narrative through imposing identity and reproducing a logic of the same (*Political Unconscious* 106). Likewise, Teresa de Lauretis characterizes genre as "institutionalized discourse" and argues that "narrative and narrativity . . . are mechanisms to be employed strategically and tactically in the effort to construct other forms of coherence" (*Technologies* 109). Narrative conventions are "technologies of gender" that both produce and reproduce existing gender relations. Rachel Blau DuPlessis has also examined the gender politics of representations. In *Writing Beyond the Ending* she describes how "romance of various kinds and the fate of female characters express attitudes at least toward family, sexuality, and gender" (x). Her study is based on the assumption that "narrative structures and subjects are like working apparatuses of ideology" and that "[n]o convention is neutral, mimetic, or purely aesthetic" (3, 2). These critics stress the connection between the textual and the social, between form and content.

Chicana postmodern vernacular texts equally resist the disjunction between art and politics implied by versions of postmodernism that follow Derridean theories. This vernacular delights in hybrid texts, where hybridity is defined as the composite of heterogeneous sources/origins whose interplay functions to juxtapose cultural practices and to denaturalize conventions. More specifically, then, this chapter attempts to demonstrate how Ana Castillo's novel *So Far From God* and Sandra Cisneros's short story "Little Miracles, Kept Promises" incorporate and deconstruct narratives that derive from diverse cultures: the European American family saga and the *telenovela* (Mexican soap operas), the short story, and Mexican American oral traditions. Through their generic hybridization, these authors, like many postmodern writers, defy notions of "generic purity" and instead offer "contaminated texts." However, they firmly root their literary transgressions in bicultural experiences. Cisneros, like Barth, ruminates on the nature of the short story genre, through the innovative visual nature of her text, which throws the traditional short story into question. These techniques capture the experiences of Mexican Americans as a constant process of negotiating two cultures while simultaneously countering Euro-centric notions in prose fiction. Their works show that discontinuities in Mexican American experience motivate experimentation and ground their fiction in historical and material reality.

Barbara Kingsolver's 1993 review of Ana Castillo's *So Far From God* draws attention to this generic hybridization when she characterizes the novel as "the offspring of a union between *One Hundred Years of Solitude* and 'General Hospital'" (1). Castillo's third novel is an outrageous tale about an untraditional Mexican American family in the New Mexico town of Tome. The story moves in circular fashion from the death and magical resurrection of one of the daughters at the beginning to her repeated death and resurrection at the end. Kingsolver's description foregrounds Castillo's combination of elements from both "high" and "low" cultures; the novel is a web of intertextual references, blending American literary and popular culture with Mexican American folklore. Castillo draws on a variety of genres, including the family saga, the *telenovela*, myth (Pueblo, Apache, and Aztec), *cuentos* (oral stories), magic realism, comedy, tragedy, folkloric elements such as *remedios* and recipes, and religious narratives.[2] Such blending of forms highlights issues of representation and of the representability of Mexican American experience in the novel form. In the following I will focus on how *So Far from God* simultaneously recalls and parodies the family saga and the *telenovela*, two genres that share concerns with family, romance, and class issues.

Family sagas such as John Galsworthy's *Forsyte Saga*, a series of three novels linked together by the Forsyte family, Thomas Mann's *Buddenbrooks* and his tetralogy *Joseph and His Brothers*, or Gabriel García Márquez's *One Hundred Years of Solitude* provide a genealogical account of a family, tracing its development through several generations and over a considerable period of time. The genre operates along a patriarchal capitalist logic: it displays a concern with social class, specifically with the preservation of the family's lineage, propriety, and decorum within the context of upper middle class values.[3] These values are brought into operation through business endeavors, and the characters' turns of fortune become a testing ground for their allegiances. Intricately related to business and enterprise is romance, and marriage is often seen as a means of ensuring or further accumulating wealth. Finally, a recurring motif is the house as symbol of the family, foregrounding notions of individual property, and reflecting an ideology of domesticity about which Ramón Saldívar writes, "domestic narratives have traditionally delineated the space of the house as a preeminent symbol of the privatized, sovereign, and individual self, plotted and fixed topographically onto a terrain of white male values" (183).

So Far From God parodies the family saga to decenter patriarchal biases inherent in the form; it further critiques individualism and constructs a new literary identity characterized by community. Like other family sagas, this novel chronicles Sofi's family over a long period of time, but this version deviates from the genre in a number of ways. Sofi's is a rather untraditional family, one that displaces patriarchy and instead celebrates a matriarchal heritage. Sofi is head of the household, house owner, and provider, while father Don Domingo is a gambler and mostly absent. Sofi and her daughters' lives form the center of the novel: Esperanza, the oldest, is a political activist and journalist; Caridad is a rural healing woman; Fe quests for the American Dream, longing for financial success and romance; and Loca is a social misfit who cannot be contained by patriarchal ideology. Sofi comments on her family's difference:

> God gave me four daughters . . . and you would have thought that by now I would be a content grandmother, sitting back and letting my daughters care for me, bringing me nothing but their babies on Sundays to rock on my lap! But no, not my hijitas! I had to produce the kind of species that flies! (84)

The novel explicitly mocks a male genealogy; Francisco, Caridad's suitor, "was the seventh son but not of a man who was the seventh son of his family"; rather, his bloodline is "crooked" (95). Fe's husband's family has seriously been "affected by the many generations of males in isolation" to the point that they have acquired the affliction of bleating (176); and doña Dolores lost all babies due to "a rare bone disease they inherited through the father's bloodline" (20).

Sofi's family is further distinguished from traditional models in that it extends beyond biological bloodlines. Whereas *Buddenbrooks*, for instance, portrays outside influences or inappropriate marriages as threatening to the family's integrity, *So Far From God* depicts the boundaries between inside and outside as highly permeable. Doña Felicia, Caridad's mentor and guide, becomes part of the family and comes to call Caridad her daughter (52). Even animals are included in Sofi's household. The novel begins with Sofi waking up "at twelve midnight to the howling and neighing of the five dogs, six cats, and four horses, whose custom it was to go freely in and out of the house" (19). Since Loca has developed an aversion for people, animals, including two dogs named after Flintstone characters Fred and Wilma, are her only and constant companions. In comic juxtapositions, family members are listed in the same breath as animals: shortly after her resurrection Loca "kept away from her other sisters, her mother, and the animals" (28).

Moreover, in contrast to the individualism reflected in the paradigmatic family saga, Castillo's version constructs a new literary identity based on collectivity by portraying the women in the family as community builders. After a series of misfortunes, Caridad, for instance, gains the community's respect by becoming a curandera, while Sofi, towards the end of the novel and in a conversation with her comadre Rita, proclaims herself mayor of Tome, only to initiate a cooperative "sheep-grazing and wool-weaving" project which ties each member of the community to all the others. The impoverished farming community collectively shares the profits from the enterprise. As we will see later on, Sofia's family is acted on by global political and economic forces, but as the founder of organizations and mayor of Tome, Sofi transforms the world around her. With this optimistic ending, Castillo defies the popular image of Mexican American women as victims of social and political forces and instead builds on their long-standing tradition of community involvement.[4] In postmodern fashion, she shows how micropolitical agencies and local forms of intervention can foster transformations from traditionally female spaces: the house, the kitchen, and the yard. Such occurrences render the ideology of domesticity—the separation of public from private sphere—defunct.[5]

So Far From God is an ironic revision of the family saga's patriarchal focus as well as its portrayal of male middle-class individuals as political personages who, due to class privilege, are major actors in the public arena. To foreground class issues, Castillo's novel engages in an intertextual dialogue with Louisa May Alcott's *Little Women*, published in 1868, and itself a revision of the family saga in that it presents a family without men. In *Little Women* Marmee wisely governs a household of four girls—Meg, Jo, Beth, and Amy. Father is absent as a chaplain in the war and appears only through his letters to the family. Since Marmee's family, like Sofi's, is poor due to a change in fortune, social class is a constant theme. Part of the girls' socialization process is to emulate the little pilgrims of Bunyan's *Pilgrim's Progress* by shouldering their burdens and forgetting about their vanities. Bunyan's Christian allegory points to the lesson the girls have to learn: to transcend poverty and the social stigma attached to it through spirituality. Marmee defines success for the girls through "energy, industry, and independence" (35). Thus Alcott's novel is a tableaux of domestic idyll; the family is a bulwark against a chaotic world characterized by war and poverty. Its fortune depends on unity; as one of the girls says, "Rich or poor, we will keep together and be happy in one another" (36).

The 1868 novel provides a foil for Sofi's family because it clarifies Castillo's project of demystifying the spiritual transcendence of poverty and dispossession as advocated by the older novel.[6] As in *Little Women*, Sofi's home is the rock that grounds the girls' existence. Even Fe, who longs to escape from what she regards as her dysfunctional family, desires to return to the house when she is dying: "Fe found herself wanting to go nowhere else but back to her mom and La Loca and even to the animals to die just before her twenty-seventh birthday. Sofi's chaotic home became a sanctuary from the even more incomprehensible world" (171–2). The rock, however, is an unstable one; the house that has been a home for Sofi's family for generations is gambled away by Don Domingo. For Sofi, the traditional value system collapses:

> Sofi had devoted her life to being a good daughter, a good wife, and a good mother, or at least had given it all a hell of a good try . . . Now there was no mother to honor, no father to respect, no 'jitas to sacrifice for, no rancho to maintain, and no land left to work. Nothing to look out for no more. (218)

Castillo quite clearly places Sofi's dispossession within the context of institutionalized ethnic and gender politics. Comadre Rita empathizes with her and adds her own story of loss,

> First the gringos took most of our land away when they took over the territory from Mexico—right after Mexico had taken it from Spain and like my vis-abuelo used to say, 'Ni

no' habiamo' dado cuenta,' it all happened so fast! Then, little by little, my familia had to
give it up 'cause they couldn't afford it no more, losing business on their churros and cattle.
(217)

In addition to colonialist dispossession, Castillo exposes the politics of marriage,
which denies Sofi individual ownership. Right after their wedding, Don Domingo
had hocked all of Sofi's jewelry that had been passed down to her through
generations. Worst of all, without so much as consulting with his wife, he had sold
ten acres of land parceled out to them by Sofi's grandfather as a wedding present.
Now that he signed away the deed to the house, Sofi ends up paying rent to a
stranger.

Sofi's family is the nexus for dramatizing dispossession and other social ills
that affect Mexican American families. They are presented in humorous and
hyperbolic fashion and without claims to realist representation. Castillo's grafting
of the conventions of the *telenovela* onto the novel allows her to suspend the
reader's disbelief. *Telenovelas*, Mexican soap operas, are a potpourri of dramatic
events, spiced with exaggeration, complications, convoluted plots, subplots, inter-
woven stories, coincidence, intrigues, and melodrama, where disaster trips
headlong into catastrophe. It is a sensationalist genre where credibility of plot and
characters are sacrificed for effect. Like a *telenovela*, the novel has an episodic
structure; each chapter/episode forms a coherent whole revolving around a major
crisis; the plot is connected through coincidence; and there are multiple subplots,
interludes, and detours.

Like characters in a *telenovela*,[7] Sofi's family undergoes all manner of plausible
and implausible transformations: Sofi is twice deserted by her husband and loses
all of her children; Esperanza, the oldest and a reporter, is killed on a mission in
Saudi Arabia; Caridad almost dies from an attack of a malogra, a mythical figure
that haunts and hurts little girls who wander too far, but experiences a "Holy
Restoration" (80). In rapid succession, she then becomes clairvoyant, lives in a
cave for a year, has a lesbian interest, and is followed by a "saint" who forces her
to take a Thelma-and-Louise-like dive off a cliff; Fe lets out a scream that lasts a
whole year after her fiancé deserts her. She quits her job at the bank and becomes
a factory worker, only to die of cancer from working with radioactive materials;
Loca is afflicted with both AIDS and epilepsy and twice rises from the dead. This
tall tale nevertheless presents a serious political and social commentary: through
both realistic and unrealistic events Castillo paints a panoramic picture of Mexican
American women in American society.[8] Castillo's novel demonstrates that life is

as outrageous for Mexican American women as fiction.

Castillo further uses conventions of the *telenovela* to parody its underlying assumptions and the normative behaviors it projects. Thematically, *telenovelas* revolve around a family and typically portray a poor but worthy girl's rise to marriage and wealth. As Antonio V. Menéndez Alarcón has argued, the *telos* of the *telenovela* is material success and heterosexual romance; he states, "Progress and social change in these shows are limited to individual access to economic power and social position" (62). The novel cleverly deflates the *telenovela*'s assumptions of romance. The title to chapter six reads, "How in '49 Sofia Got Swept Off Her Feet by Domingo's Clark Gable Mustache" (103). The following chapter, however, presents an ironic inversion of romance; after focusing on Sofi and Domingo's budding love affair, young Sofi's high expectations, and the couple's elopement, it foregrounds their subsequent estrangement produced by his gambling and escape. Their life together is described in rather anti-climactic terms: "They acted like a couple who had actually been together for the better part of their nearly 35-year marriage and had become so used to each other that they didn't even notice one another no more, like an old chair in the corner of the room" (109).

Most importantly, the novel critiques the idea of individual progress through the character of Fe who, like Alcott's little pilgrims, longs to shape her life into a success story and to lift herself up from her *familia* through her work ethic. Her sense of reality derives from popular culture, and, as Fe herself professes, she desires nothing more than to "have a life like people do on TV" (189). The novel depicts a succession of tragic failures, as she is jilted by her fiancé, demoted by the Savings and Loans, and betrayed by Acme International, the company that ironically recalls the one from which the cartoon character Wile E. Coyote obtains an array of explosives in his pursuit of the Road Runner. Finally, and in contrast to the promise of social status and acclaim through wealth, the novel inverts the *telenovela*'s paradigm of the good person who triumphs at the end by elevating Loca, the social outcast and androphobe. After her death from AIDS, Sofi founds yet another organization for Mothers of Martyrs and Saints (M.O.M.A.S.), and people revere Loca as a saint.[9] As she exposes the family saga's reproduction of patriarchal and capitalist ideologies, Castillo critiques the *telenovela*'s social function as, in Elizabeth Lozano's words, "pedagogical and enculturating discourse," as facilitators for social development (207).

As *So Far From God* takes liberties with the novel form, Cisneros experiments

with the short story. "Little Miracles, Kept Promises," her most frequently
anthologized piece of prose fiction, constructs a dialogue between the written
short story genre and Mexican American oral traditions to focus on the
discontinuities in the lives of Chicanos/as. In an interview with Reed Way
Dasenbrook and Feroza Jussawalla, Cisneros has suggested her interest in
innovation, "I'm just not taken by the linear novel form, . . . I'm much more
interested in something new happening to literature" (304). And so she turns to
the short story, a "minor" genre, in Mary Louise Pratt's terms, which, according
to Pratt, has greater potential for experimentation in subject-matter and style
precisely because of its status as a lesser genre ("The Short Story" 181; 187).
Renato Rosaldo, speaking of short story cycles, echoes this assessment: "Their
'formal marginality' . . . enables them to become arenas for experimentation, the
development of alternative visions . . . Marginal genres thus are often the site of
political innovation and cultural creativity." ("Fables" 88). And indeed, imagistic
episodic vignettes have become the hallmark of Cisneros's fiction.[10]

"Little Miracles" differs from more traditional short stories with their linear
plot development and conflict-resolution structure in that it is plotless; it has no
central narrator or character and is made up of twenty-three peticiónes, pleading
notes people leave together with small gifts in churches to request saintly
intervention. The title signals that the story derives from the Mexican and Mexican
American "ex-voto" (Latin for "from my vow") tradition. Catholic churches in the
Rio Grande Valley display numerous ex-votos or milagros, images and small gifts
created most commonly out of tin, paper, or wood. They are hung by the shrines
of saints as a sign of gratitude for answered prayers. No narrative commentary
frames the notes, and only the shrines provide the structural center that connects
them.

Through its large cast of characters and polyphony of voices, the story
explodes the unity of impression characteristic of Poe-esque short stories, and at
the same time challenges constructions of a singular and homogeneous Chicano
subject; rather, these petitions reflect heterogeneity through the multiplicity of
concerns and tensions evident in the lives of Chicanas and Chicanos. Each note
provides a moment, a glimpse, and is highly provisional. Taken together, the
vignettes present a panoramic picture of Mexican American culture in rural and
poverty-stricken South Texas. Barbara Harlowe's observation that Cisneros's *House
on Mango Street* is filled with "stories which recount the short histories of the
neighborhood's inhabitants embedded in the larger history of Hispanic

immigration, relocation, and political displacement in the U.S." (161), curiously fits this story as well.

Much of the effect of "Little Miracles" derives from the discrepancy between the formality commonly associated with prayers and the every-day language in which the characters articulate their desires to the saints. The prayers reveal a multiplicity of tones, ranging from serious to comic and reflecting the characters' different predicaments. While a grandmother prays for the healing of her two-year-old cancer-stricken granddaughter, another petitioner writes,

> Saint Jude, patron saint of lost causes,
>> Help me pass my English 320, British Restoration Literature class and everything to turn out ok.
>>> Eliberto Gonzáles, Dallas. (124)

Or here is the fierce voice of Ms. Barbara Ybañes, who ends her note with a "manda," a "promise" to the saint unless he grants her wish:

> Dear San Antonio de Padua,
>> Can you please help me find a man who isn't a pain in the nalgas. There aren't any in Texas, I swear. Especially not in San Antonio. . . .
>> I'll turn your statue upside down until you send him to me. (117–8)

The story's focus on voice and its creation of Mexican American characters through their linguistic habits constitutes an attempt at capturing Chicano/a vernacular speech and infuses the text with an oral quality.[11] Other stylistic features help to recreate this oral quality. The above excerpts show the linguistic code-switching characteristic of Mexican American speech, as do Fito Moroles's words, "Thank you por el milagro de haber graduado de high school" (123). Lack of punctuation in one note results in a Joycean interior monologue. Use of caps in another signals Leocadia's desperate outcry for the healing of her granddaughter. Informal sentence structures, slang, dialectal use of pronouns, and expletives further capture the sounds of oral speech, as in "Oh Seven African Powers, come on, don't be so bad. Let my Illinois Lottery ticket win" (119). Further, the use of apostrophe in the form of direct addresses of the saints creates the immediacy of interpersonal communication.

Cisneros's recreation of the phonetic and syntactic patterns of spoken language aligns "Little Miracles" with oral and ethnopoetic traditions, specifically that of the *declamadores*, speakers/actors who recite and perform an author's work.

This tradition finds easier transmission in poetry and plays, as in Carmen Tafolla's poem "Los Corts (5 Voices)," written in five monologues, and in Denise Chávez's short play *Novena Narrativas y Ofrendas Nuevomexicanas*, nine introspective personal narrations by Mexican American characters of different ages and backgrounds. Similar to Cisneros's story, Chávez's monologues revolve around the Virgin and record the characters' "hopes, dreams, and devotions" (85). Nonetheless, the large cast of characters, the series of monologues, and creation of characters through their voices provide Cisneros's informal notes with a dramatic quality.[12] In the declamatory tradition, the pieces *perform* the voices of Mexican Americans, their hopes, and their sorrows as they come to pray at the shrine. Through their narrations, these characters become authors of their stories, exert agency, and validate their experiences. As a result of capturing their voices, the story deconstructs dominant ideological discourses of Mexican Americans as mere victims of society.

The story's multiple character-narrators require a constant repositioning on the part of the reader due to the gaps between letters, shifts from speaker to speaker, and new locations. Each piece in itself reveals, upon close reading, many hidden tensions. For instance, Arnulfo Contreras's plea that the Tortillería la Casa de la Masa pay him the $253.72 they owe him for two weeks' work reveals the exploitative conditions many Mexican Americans suffer in a capitalist economy that uses them as cheap labor (he made less than $2 an hour). Similarly, Adelfa Vásquez's prayer is symptomatic of conflict:

> Please send us clothes, furniture, shoes, dishes. We need anything that don't eat. Since the fire we have to start all over again and Lalo's disability check ain't much and don't go far. Zulema would like to finish school but I says she can just forget about it now. She's our oldest and her place is at home helping us out I told her. Please make her see some sense. She's all we got. (117)

Here, the economic hardship of life in the borderlands clashes with the promise of the American Dream and education for all. The letter specifically calls attention to the situation of some Mexican American girls who as teenagers perform maternal functions for the rest of the family.

The very short final petition is preceded by a monologue, the voice of Rosario De Leon, who brings the offering of a braid of her hair. Rosario's internal monologue disrupts the flow of the piece—it sets a halt to the prayers we have become accustomed to reading and draws attention to the margins and gaps between the petitions, and to the processes, conflicts, and negotiations behind the product. The subject of the monologue is one woman's self-reflexive negotiation with the dual cultures she lives in. She attempts to come to terms with the Virgin of Guadalupe, herself a blending between Spanish and Indian traditions, and an icon that speaks to the construction of racial, cultural, and gender identity. Rosario rejects the self-sacrifice the Virgin seems to demand: "I couldn't see you without seeing my ma each time my father came home drunk and yelling, blaming everything that ever went wrong in his life on her. I couldn't look at your folded hands without seeing my *abuela* mumbling, 'My son, my son, my son'" (127).

In her desire to reinvent herself, a process which Cisneros describes elsewhere as "taking from tradition that which nurtures and abandoning the element which would mean our self-destruction" ("I Can Live" 5), Rosario breaks up the monolithic image of the Virgin and revises her as Aztec warrior queen:

> I wanted you bare-breasted, snakes in your hands. I wanted you leaping and somersaulting the backs of bulls. I wanted you swallowing raw hearts and rattling volcanic ash. I wasn't going to be my mother or my grandma. All that self-sacrifice, all that silent suffering. Hell no. Not here. Not me. (127)

The invocation of the snake, suggesting earth-boundedness in the symbology of the Nahuatl, the Mexican and central Indian tribes of which the Aztecs were one, contrasts with the spirituality the Virgin of Guadalupe represents. Rosario's process of negotiation ends with insight:

> How I finally understood who you are. No longer Mary the mild, but our mother Tonantzín. That you could have the power to rally a people when a country was born, and again during civil war, and during a farmworkers' strike in California made me think maybe there is power in my mother's patience, strength in my grandmother's endurance. (128)

Rosario superimposes Mexica goddesses onto images of the Virgin, such as Tonantzín (earth goddess), Tlazolteotl (goddess of carnal sin, love, and confession), or Coatlicue (earth goddess) and juxtaposes them with the Spanish Nuestra Señora de los Remedios and Nuestra Señora del Perpetua Socorro.[13] Thus Rosario comes to understand the Guadalupe as a syncretic construct, one that signals both self-sacrifice and resistance against dominant ideology and imperialism. In the process, Rosario appropriates and brings together a jumble of cultural allusions that points out the constructed nature of myths and that is at the same time symptomatic of mestiza consciousness. Rosario concludes, "I wasn't ashamed then, to be my mother's daughter, my grandmother's granddaughter, my ancestor's child" (128). In the words of Jean Wyatt: "Rosario rejects Guadalupe, re-examines her, embraces her, and finally reconstructs her as a figure that she can understand, live with, and use as a model. To revise the traditional icons is to empower oneself" (266).

These two Chicana texts illustrate the constant process of revision, mediation, negotiation, and transformation dictated by life on the border. Straddling two antithetical cultures means, in Pat Mora's poem "Legal Alien," "sliding back and forth/between the fringes of both worlds" (*Chants* 60), an enabling and oppressive movement that exemplifies the postmodern condition where unitary systems of values or stable centers of reference no longer exist and the creation of new ideologies and genres is imperative. I read these texts as postmodern double-voiced and palimpsestic discourses, speaking from both sides of the border and signifying the dialectic relationship among Mexican (ethnic) and other traditions to express the multiple identities of Chicana *mestizaj*e. Castillo's novel and Cisneros's short story are inclusive works, texts that incorporate and include, that write through and across the social, political, and cultural forces that work against Mexican Americans. Their blending of genres—family saga and telenovela, and short story and *tradición declamar*—suggests a blending of cultures, histories, and epistemes.

In the process, *So Far From God* and "Little Miracles" also modify mainstream theoretical paradigms of postmodernism as an aesthetic and ahistorical practice. While postmodernism's emphasis on the local, the margins, and difference has created spaces for Chicanas to speak from, Chicana writing, together with that of other women and people of color, has contributed to creating a multicultural, political version of postmodernism. These pieces of prose fiction depict radical experimentation yet no ahistorical play of signifier. Both texts foreground historical discontinuities that characterize Chicana literature and that account for its textual disruptions. A consideration of these Chicana texts within the framework of postmodernism undoes the all-too-familiar binary opposition between aesthetics and politics, between postmodernism and political engagement.

Chapter 5

Desert Women, *Brujas,* and *Curanderas*: Pat Mora's Linguistic *Mestizaje*

> The problem with binary thinking: terms are defined by what they are not. Languages are opposed in pairs, and to be bilingual is to switch codes from one to the other, not to mix them. Anything less than a complete jump from one pole to the other is termed "interference" in this way of thinking, with the negative connotations the word carries. The space between the languages is the forbidden zone of neither this nor that. Those who practice a type of speech located in the zone of mixture are linguistic outlaws for the purists at either pole.
>
> Juan Bruce-Novoa, "A Case of Identity" (33).

Instinctively exclaiming *"Ay!",* explains the narrator of Sandra Cisneros's short story *"Bien* Pretty," is the true test of a native Spanish speaker, and she continues,

> To make love in Spanish, in a manner as intricate and devout as the Alhambra. To have a lover sigh *mi vida, mi preciosa, mi chiquitita,* and whisper things in that language crooned to babies, that language murmured by grandmothers, those words that smelled like your house, like flour tortillas, and the inside of your daddy's hat, like everyone talking in the kitchen at the same time, or sleeping with the windows open . . .
>
> *That* language. That sweep of palm leaves and fringed shawls. That startled fluttering, like the heart of a goldfinch or a fan. Nothing sounded dirty or hurtful or corny. How could I think of making love in English again? English with its starched r's and g's. English with its crisp linen syllables. English crunchy as apples, resilient and stiff as sailcloth.
>
> But Spanish whirled like silk, rolled and puckered and hissed. (153–4)

In this excerpt from Cisneros's story, the binary opposition between English and Spanish Juan Bruce-Novoa discusses in the above epigraph, is clearly at work. Each language carries different associations for the narrator. Spanish, in this story, is the language of the private domain of love, the sonorous language of poetry as it "rolls, puckers, and hisses," the language of the familial realm, the language of comfort and security in the home, and the language nostalgically associated with childhood. The use of the Spanish language also evokes a larger matrix of culture and place: the phrase "the sweep of palm leaves" in the second paragraph indicates a connection to a Southern geography, and "fringed shawls" indicates a connection with Mexican culture. The English language, in contrast, is seen as alien territory; words like "starched," "crisp," and "stiff" indicate not only unfamiliarity but constraint, lack of ease, and lack of expressiveness.

Such reflections on English and Spanish are common in Chicana literature. Through these, Cisneros dramatizes the artist/narrator Lupe as a displaced person, both geographically and linguistically, as she moves from California to Texas. The move serves to reconnect her with her Mexican heritage and results in an affair with Flavio, who, in her view, represents the embodiment of mexicanidad. Lupe's initial nativist nostalgia finds expression in her turn to classical Mexican motifs in her painting and in her veneration of the Spanish language as a marker of ethnicity. However, the linguistic texture of the passage as well as the intrasentential code-switching in the story's title, "*Bien* Pretty," radically undercuts Lupe's claims to authentic Mexicanness. The very dominance of English in this passage points to the U.S. American part of her roots, which Lupe finally acknowledges as the story comes to a close.

Through the interplay between English and Spanish, Chicana (and Chicano) writers are, in Juan Bruce-Novoa's words, the "linguistic outlaws" who explore the forbidden zone, blur the boundaries between binary oppositions, and delve into the spaces between languages. Like poststructuralists, they reject linguistic purists bent on keeping English and Spanish in separate textual universes. They are the linguistic mestizas, mixing not just standard English and Spanish, but throwing in the vernaculars typical of the U.S.-Mexico border region: caló, Tejano English, and popular Spanish. They thus present another instance of what Bill Ashcroft, Gareth Griffiths, and Helen Tiffin call "english," the variations of standard English across the world and of "the language of the erstwhile imperial centre" (8). Frances R. Aparicio calls attention to Latino/a writers' linguistic experimentalism and describes its various forms as "tropicalization." The term refers to the writers' transformation of English from within (796), through lexical and syntactical innovations. Traditionally associated with uneducated speakers, *calques*, for example, the literal translation of Spanish constructions into English, offer opportunities for innovation and experimentalism. Aparicio suggests, "the most important contributions of U.S. Latino/a writers to American literature lie . . . in the new possibilities for metaphors, imagery, syntax, and rhythm that the Spanish subtexts provide literary English" (797). While some may see the use of *calques* or of code-switching as a deficit, Aparicio suggests that "a postmodern . . . approach would validate it as a positively creative innovation in literature" (797).

This chapter engages the issue of interlingualism—its linguistic as well as its social aspects, both of which are highlighted in Cisneros's quote—to show intersections with postmodern and poststructuralist disruptions of binary thinking. Specifically, interlingualism is an instance of linguistic innovation that raises important questions: If linguistic experimentation is the hallmark of postmodern literature, what is the place of bilingual and bicultural authors' interlingualism on this scene? What are the connections and disconnections between postmodern and Chicano/a concepts of linguistic experimentation? What are the limits of poststructuralist theory in understanding interlingualism? To answer these questions, I examine the work of Pat Mora—poet, essayist, and author of children's books—who, like many Chicana authors, writes English-dominant poetry and prose but frequently transgresses linguistic boundaries through the inclusion of Spanish in her work.[1] I argue that poststructuralist theory of linguistic play and transgression has limited explanatory value. To fully understand interlingualism in Mora's work, one must look at the socio-historical field into which language use is embedded, specifically taking into account that in a U.S. American context, not all languages are created equal and that Spanish has been heavily suppressed in the Southwestern states. As a poetic strategy, code-switching seeks to question and undermine monolingualism and monoculturalism as it creates a dialogue between two worlds. Linguistic code-switching *in print*, then, is a way of validating the experiences of those who are marginalized in American society. It is a form of linguistic experimentalism that is historically grounded in the author's bicultural heritage. Linguistic *mestizaje* hence is the purview of writers in the borderlands, authors who live in this middle country, betwixt and between two stable identities, antithetical world views, and literary practices.

Linguistic experimentation is often regarded as the hallmark of postmodernism. Theorists such as Allen Thiher, Brian McHale, Raymond Federman, and others have shaped views of postmodern experimentation as consisting of transgressive language games. Experimental texts break up the linguistic system through verbal play, deferral of meaning, and disruptions of syntax. Such theories resist Aristotelian views of language as nomenclature, where words are the reflections of the mind and the soul and where the relationship between language and the world is unproblematic and natural. Words, in this view, represent objects, and language functions as the agent of communication. Because this theory regards language as a transparent medium, Catherine Belsey explains, "it is characteristic of language to be overlooked" (42).

In contrast, language gains primary importance in the Derridean project of dismantling traditional Western thought. In the wake of theorists such as Ludwig Wittgenstein, Martin Heidegger, and Ferdinand de Saussure, Derrida challenges a representational view of language. These authors emphasize the arbitrary and differential nature of signs, the autonomy of the linguistic system, the speaker's subjection to the rules of language, and language's articulation or construction rather than reflection of the world. For the purposes of this discussion, two concepts are important: Derrida's theories of *différance* and of translation.

Derrida's influential and programmatic essay "Différance" perhaps best describes his view of the functioning of language. *Différance*—a linguistic innovation that simultaneously suggests "to differ" and "to defer"—highlights that language is constituted "as a weave of differences" ("Différance" 12). As he explains elsewhere, a text is "a differential network, a fabric of traces referring endlessly to something other than itself, to other differential traces" ("Living On" 84). Many poststructuralist texts perform Derrida's theory of an endless deferral of meaning. As we saw in chapter one, Derrida's own "Living On: BORDER LINES," presents his ruminations on the interplay between Percy Bysshe Shelley's *Triumph of Life* and Maurice Blanchot's *Arrêt de Mort* and is a performative display of language's polysemic and self-generative properties—a metaphoric translation of the terms of the one text (triumph/life) into the language of the other (arrest/death). He suggests that meanings always spill over so that each text gets caught up in the language of the other (triumph/arrest; life/death; "Living On" 123). Derrida focuses on "the open polysemia of Blanchot's title that plays with the language to the point of stopping [*arrêter*] any translation of it" ("Living On" 109). This polysemia resides in the semantic instability of the French *arrêt*, suggesting two irreconcilable meanings—a judgment that arrests (death sentence) or the suspension of death. Any *Aufhebung* (synthesis) is impossible; there is only indecision of meaning ("Living On" 115). Derrida engages in similar play with his own title, juxtaposing "living" and "living on" (*vivre* and *survivre*), which are in a relation "not of clear-cut opposition nor of stable equivalence"; instead, "'living, living on' differs and defers, like '*différance*,' beyond identity and difference" ("Living On" 136). Thus Derrida resists arresting meaning, since any such arrest is arbitrary and a death sentence to free play.

Much of Derrida's work is particularly relevant to a discussion of Chicana literature since it focuses on issues of translation, not just metaphoric translation of the language of one text into that of another, but translation from one national language into another. He demonstrates how the interplay of two or more languages opens up texts to more radical verbal play. Like the cross-fertilization between texts, such ludic activity contributes to a proliferation of meaning. Other poststructuralists have used these techniques as well. For instance, Jean-Luc Nancy's reflections on *mestizaje* brings in French meanings and resonances of the term *metissage*, which, re-translated into English, gives rise to his title "Cut-Throat Sun." On a more theoretical note, Derrida takes issue with classical models of translation that assume a "transportable univocality" ("BORDER LINES" 93). His concept of dissemination clashes with the idea that national languages are made up of "semantic radicals properly bordered" ("BORDER LINES" 119–20). This model, he argues, in fact neutralizes language ("BORDER LINES" 94). Translation, then, is never problem-free. It always fixes meaning, arrests movement, and leaves out possible significations ("BORDER LINES"118). For example, when Blanchot's *L'Arrêt de Mort* is translated into English as "Death Sentence," it closes off the opposite meaning, "suspension of death," which could also be generated and can only be put back into play by the bilingual reader. In "Freud and the Scene of Writing," Derrida explains, "translation . . . presupposes a text which would be there, immobile . . . the serene presence of a statue, or of a written stone or archive whose signified content might be harmlessly transported into the milieu of a different language" (211). Thus semantic stability, translation, and grammar are all part of the order of law, and of authority, which delimits freedom and presumes an illusory purity.

A postmodern/poststructuralist perspective helps highlight interlingualism in Chicana literature as a play of signification and experimental transgression, or, in Derridean terms, an "overrun" of the borders of one language into another. Poststructuralism thus provides a useful framework for thinking about linguistic *mestizaje*: first, it helps see how language creates reality. Derrida's reflections on translation question the assumption of language literally transposing or replacing signified contents. As Gloria Anzaldúa has stated in an interview with Andrea Lunsford, "the language, this particular symbolic system . . . displaces the reality, the experience, so that you take the language to be the reality" (65). English and Spanish are more than tools for communication; they represent different ways of ordering reality.

Second, the interplay between languages creates a rich field of reference and cross-reference where bilingual readers, able to decipher how Spanish subtexts govern the English surface, will be at an advantage. Consider, for instance, the title of another one of Cisneros's short stories, "Salvador Late or Early," which illustrates this complexity. Most obviously, the title refers to the vignette's central character named Salvador, who is "late or early," a literal translation (*calque*) of the Spanish phrase "tarde o temprano." Bilingual readers will also know that the boy is symbolically named since "salvador" means "savior." These readers might find this an important contextual clue to the character, an abused child who takes care of his siblings. They might also read "late" as a form of the Spanish verb *latir* referring to the heart's beat. *Salvador late* then suggests that Salvador/savior/the Savior lives, that there is a Savior for little boys like Salvador, that many little boys are saviors like him. As Bruce-Novoa has it, interlingual literature "exploit[s] and create[s] the potential conjunctions of interconnection," resulting in a different code ("Spanish-Language Loyalty" 49), a hybrid language where unmarked blending is the norm. Third, and last, interlingualism constitutes a defiance of the law of grammaticality; it is an expression against purism, against partition, and against stable categories.

Poststructuralism, in particular its focus on the signifying potential of language and its ability to generate multiple meanings, thus has great analytical value. However, in this call to "defy the law" from within language itself, Derrida does not engage in specifics to indicate what it is, exactly, that must be challenged. In his discussion of framing and creating borders he vaguely states that literary institutions are built on framing ("BORDERLINES" 88), but avoids asking who does the framing? Who sets the terms? Who sets up partitions and who benefits from inclusion/exclusion? Like a monolingual reader, poststructuralism reacts only to linguistic surfaces and decontextualizes debates behind language use.

Poststructuralist materialists Gilles Deleuze and Félix Guattari link language a bit more specifically to issues of domination and power. In their view, grammaticality is a marker of power and prerequisite for submission to social laws. They suggest "deterritorializing" (*A Thousand* 106) the major language through a minor language, as Kafka did with German or as Chicanos/as do with standard English. The goal is to "use the minor language to send the major language racing" (105–6). As in Derrida's work, the emphasis is on the inherent revolutionary potential of language itself.

I propose that a closer examination of the relation between Spanish and English in the United States—a relation that has been fraught with conflict—gives insight into writers' uses of the languages. I draw on one of the basic tenets of sociolinguistics, that language cannot be separated from its usage; language is always tied to social practices.[2] This approach stresses the need to step outside of the system of language and look at the social context of the relation between English and Spanish in a specific location, the U.S., at a specific time in history.

The systematic suppression of Spanish in the Southwestern U.S. provides an important context for understanding code-switching in literature. From 1848 onward, European Americans imposed not only systems of government and a class structure but also their own culture and their language. They tried, unsuccessfully, to erase Spanish. As Bruce-Novoa explains, "From the first encounter between Spanish-speaking inhabitants and the foreigners who spoke, among other languages, English, the history of Texas, like that of the country itself, has been marked by efforts to eliminate Spanish from the conquered territories and impose English as the official language" ("Spanish-Language Loyalty" 41). The Derridean notions of free play and intertranslation, then, are severely restricted by regulations and legislation meant to suppress Spanish.

An example of such legislation is Bill no. 128 from the Texas State Legislature, introduced, according to historian Rudolph Anthony Quiroz, in the wake of Americanization movements and attempts to homogenize society (198). The law went into effect on June 27, 1918 and is worth quoting at length, not in the least because it provided detailed provisions for its enforcement:

> Section 1. Every teacher, principal, and superintendent employed in the public free schools of this state shall use the English language exclusively in the conduct of the work of the schools, and all recitations and exercises of the school shall be conducted in the English language, and the trustees shall not prescribe any texts for elementary grades not printed in the English language; provided, that this provision shall not prevent the teaching of Latin, Greek, French, German, Spanish, Bohemian, or other language as a branch of study in the high school grades as outlined in the state course of study.
> Section 2. Any teacher, principal, superintendent, trustee, or other school official having responsibility in the conduct of the work of the school, and failing to comply with this provision of the law shall be deemed guilty of misdemeanor and upon conviction thereof in proper court shall be subject to fine [sic] of no less than Twenty-five Dollars ($ 25.00) and not more than One Hundred Dollars ($ 100.00), cancellation of certificate, or removal from office as the case may be, or both fine and removal from office. Each day shall be regarded as a separate offense, and it shall be the duty of the trustee, city or county superintendent, or ex-officio superintendent to inspect the schools regularly with regard to the enforcement of this Act and file charges promptly in the court in all cases of violation. (Quoted from Quiroz 199).

The effects of this restriction are obvious in such enculturating institutions as schools. Aída Hurtado and Raúl Rodríguez have studied South Texas school

districts with large numbers of Spanish-dominant students which adopted a No
Spanish Rule even *after* 1968. Infractions often led to physical punishment of
students and indictments of teachers violating the rule (404). Ana Celia Zentella
goes so far as to claim that the greatest efforts made to the restrict language in the
U.S. since the post-World War I period have been taking place *since* 1980 (71). She
shows employers' uses of similar tactics of punishment and termination of workers
for speaking Spanish in other workplaces (77–78).[3] It is not surprising, then, that
observations such as Gloria Anzaldúa's are common in Chicana literature.
Anzaldúa remembers,

> . . . being caught speaking Spanish at recess—that was good for three licks on the knuckles
> with a sharp ruler. I remember being sent to the corner of the classroom for "talking back"
> to the Anglo teacher when all I was trying to do was tell her how to pronounce my name.
> If you want to be American, speak 'American.' If you don't like it, go back to Mexico
> where you belong. (*Borderlands* 53)[4]

Anzaldúa's comments illustrate the repression of Spanish, but they also imply the
strong symbolic connection between language and nationhood. Speaking Spanish
is considered a betrayal, a sign of being "un-American." Studies focusing on
attitudes towards the Spanish language support this claim. Nancy Sullivan and
Robert Schatz, for example, discuss the symbolism inherent in English Language
Legislation (ELL) debates (271).[5] They find strong evidence of nationalistic
attitudes and prejudice against non-Europeans among the supporters of ELL
(272). Similarly, Zentella speaks of the "[b]latent hispanophobia" (74) inherent in
the English Only movement. Anti-Spanish attitudes, she explains, "flourish when
Latino language and culture is viewed as unequal and undemocratic, and
monolithic" (76). Mexican Americans are perceived as a group that will not easily
assimilate.[6] One could argue that quite literally then, code-switching challenges the
English Only movement and the laws and propositions it advances, including
English Language Legislation.

As a result of these tensions, "[a] Mexican American author's relationship to
standard English is a political one" (53), as critic María Gonzáles categorically
announces. Similarly, Rosaura Sánchez states that "Chicano discourse must be seen
in light of a macro-socio-historical framework" (*Chicano Discourse* 92). Within this
restrictive context, it is inevitable for language, as Ada Savin puts it, to become the
"battle horse in a realm where power relations are at work" (216). To counter the
colonization of the Spanish language, Anzaldúa advocates recuperating Spanish

and incorporating it into the English text. As we saw in chapter two, in her definition of mestiza consciousness, revision, redefinition, and validation are important terms (82). For her, linguistic code-switching becomes a "counter-terrorist attack" that challenges a monologic worldview, nationalistic and purist ideals, and racist attitudes.[7]

But code-switching has long had a stigma attached to it, and its viability is, as Bruce-Novoa has pointed out, denied by purists from *either* language ("Spanish-Language Loyalty" 49). As Delfina Silva Cardillo reports, it is frequently regarded as a "sad linguistic phenomenon" even by those who practice it. Similarly, Letticia D. Galindo concludes her study of Laredo women speaking Border Spanish, an amalgam of Spanish and English, as follows: "[t]he innovativeness and pragmatic value of code-switching, the creation of new lexical forms borrowed from English and created through Spanish morphology, and the unique caló lexicon were not recognized as such by the majority of the women" (16). Indeed, many of the women regarded their own language choices as deficient and harbored linguistic insecurities about not speaking the "correct" version of either English or Spanish. Whereas poststructuralists would celebrate their innovative use of language, the women in the study perceived it as deviance from the norm (ie. standard English and standard Spanish). Purist attitudes such as these are at odds with the very make-up of English or Spanish, denying the dynamic nature and assimilative properties of language.

By the same token, linguists have long regarded intersentential code-switching as "interference," as Bruce-Novoa mentions in the epigraph. However, reevaluations of the phenomenon began in the early 1970s.[8] Jan Blom and John Gumpertz's study first took code-switching seriously and found highly predictable indicators for language shifts. In contrast to the Laredo women, they present code-switching as a "skilled performance" governed by strict rules. However, some attempts to explain code-switching between English and Spanish tend to be unduly deterministic and don't account for the *effects* created by language shifts. Like Cisneros's Lupe, for whom the Spanish language indicates authentic *mexicanidad*, some models relate the amount of Spanish in writers' works to their degree of identification with Mexico. In *Chicano Discourse,* Sánchez, for example, values bilingualism largely for its preservation of the Spanish language. Her paradigm of biculturalism is based on degrees of assimilation expressed in a movement from stable bilingualism (Spanish dominant with some English) to dynamic, transitional, and vestigial bilingualism (English dominant with some Spanish). The argument runs that the higher the degree of assimilation, the greater the loss of the Spanish language. Such scales tend to privilege, in classic Marxist fashion, stable bilingualism, characteristic, as Sanchez finds, of mostly working class Mexican Americans. I find her glorification of the working class as the only preserver of unadulterated, "true" Mexican culture troubling. Such a model of Chicano discourse, when translated to a bilingual poetics, can easily become prescriptive and highly evaluative, where authors who use "more" Spanish phrases, are the most "truly Chicano" writers. María Gonzáles advances a similar argument and distinguishes among the cultural assimilationist, cultural accomodationist, and revisionist use of standard English, only the latter of which gains her favor due to its disruption and abandonment of standard forms. Again, the best, or most "Chicano" writer is the least acculturated one.[9] In contrast, Mora's poetry, as I hope to demonstrate, highlights the effects that even sparse use of Spanish, when strategically inserted into the text, can have.

More useful, I believe, is Eva Mendieta-Lombardo and Zaida A. Cintron's study, which uses Carol Myers-Scotton's markedness model to analyze code-switching in bilingual Latino poetry. According to this model, there are two uses of code-switching, "emblematic" and "realistic." "Emblematic" code-switching is Shana Poplack's term for the use of culturally loaded Spanish words that are connected to ethnic identity is, such as "mi vida, mi preciosa, mi chiquitita" in the above excerpt by Cisneros. In general conversation, they constitute a marked choice, that is, a language choice that draws attention to itself. "Realistic" code-switching, on the other hand, is when a language shift is used according to the rules of oral communication among bilingual peers and constitutes an unmarked choice. However, in a formal context such as literature, Mendieta-Lombardo and Cintron argue, code-switching is always a radical moment of foregrounding. "Emblematic code-switching" becomes the unmarked choice, and "realistic code-switching" is the marked choice.

Mora's work contains many examples of both emblematic and realistic code-switching. Through emblematic code-switching, Mora frequently evokes a world of women rooted in their culture and in the land. As do the writings of other Chicanas, Mora's portrays the world of *abuelas*, which in many of her poems is the only Spanish word. "Abuelita Magic" (*Chants* 41), for instance, focuses on a grandmother who heals her daughter and new baby with sleep by preparing a rattle out of a dried red chiles. The grandmother, a "gray-haired shaman," represents the learned wisdom, the ritual, the one who finds solutions in the land.[10] A similar power based on female traditions of curing and healing is evident in "Curandera" (*Chants* 32–3) and "The Old Crone" (*Communion* 82). In Mora's depiction of the Mexican American archetype of the curandera, desert and woman become one. The faith healer leads a deeply spiritual life and "wakes early, lights candles before/her sacred statues, brews tea of *yerbabuena*" (32), a clear emblematic reference to her world. The same feminine principles of nurturing and mothering are found in the desert landscape. In the many parallel constructions in "Mi Madre" (*Chants* 14–5), the speaker invokes the desert's various powers to feed her, tease her, frighten her, and heal her. The desert is personified as a mother that provides for her: "She gives me *manzanilla, orégano, dormilón*" (14). Mora uses Spanish phrases to produce just the effects Mendieta-Lombardo and Cintron's theory predicts, "to engage the reader through the evocation of cultural images that are intimately connected with the Hispanic identity" (568). However, an exclusive focus on emblematic code-switching, I would argue, can carry the danger of foregrounding the characters' exoticism and Otherness.

The second factor in Mendieta-Lombardo and Cintron's model, "realistic" code-switching creates verisimilitude by reflecting the linguistic realities of bicultural individuals. Clearly, the point of some of Mora's poems is to mirror the social and linguistic realities of her characters. She does so in a series of poems that deal with first generation migrants—their primary identification with Mexico and with Spanish. "Village Therapy" (*Chants* 40), "Puesta del Sol" (*Chants* 28), and "The Loving Strip" (*Agua Santa* 3–4) are elegiac descriptions of ordinary people char-acterized as Mexican through quoted speeches in Spanish. For example, "The Loving Strip" focuses on the generation gap between first-generation Mexican Americans and second. While Aunt Lobo is outraged at the promiscuity on popular TV, the children enjoy it and tease her. At the end of the day, she blesses them: "Late at night, she lifted her hand above / our bodies, 'La cruz más grande del mundo.' / Her blessing, a sturdy, familiar quilt" (3). Similarly, quoted Spanish phrases help to characterize and validate the lives of Mexican workers in a series of poems about Mexican household workers. For instance, in "Graduation Morning" (*Chants* 34) the worker, who daily crosses the Rio Grande to clean houses, calls the boy of the woman she works for "lucero," bright star, an expression of the love and pride she feels in a child not her own. "*Lucero, mi lucero,*" she cries out when she sees him. On the morning of his graduation, while "Tears slide down her wrinkled cheeks," the author uses the epithet of endearment for the *woman*: "Her eyes, *luceros*, stroke his face." This authorial reversal places emphasis on the worker's generosity.

The problem with Mendieta-Lombardo and Cintron's model is its structuralist reliance on the binary opposition marked/unmarked, which generates only two ways of using code-switching, "emblematic" and "realistic." Apart from the fact that it can be difficult to distinguish between the two, there may very well be different ways of employing this linguistic strategy. As "Graduation Morning" suggests, a *poetics* of code-switching assumes that language shifts are strategically placed rhetorical tools that create certain effects. When the Spanish phrases are not clearly emblematic and do not appear in quotation marks identifying them as speeches, or are unmarked by italics, as in Mora's later collections of poetry, the reading experience is, I would argue, much more disruptive.[11] This type of code-switching supports Anzaldúa statement that interlingualism "jerks the reader out of his world and makes her think" by confronting her with another (Lunsford 71). It makes great demands on the audience's flexibility and creates a much more interactive text. It also allows the author to indicate through the interaction of languages something about the interaction of cultures. In the following, I will trace that interaction in two groups of poems, those that present powerful effects of linguistic displacement and insecurity on the individual psyche, and poems that reflect upon historic relations among inhabitants of the U.S.-Mexico borderlands and seek to "heal" the divides.

In the first group of poems Mora zooms in on the effects of historical wounds on the individual psyche—a necessary step before healing takes place. Two poems explore the isolation and separation of the transplanted Mexican monolingual individual. The first, "Elena" (*Chants* 58), contains the presumably translated monologue of a Mexican mother who now fails to understand her children due to her lack of proficiency in English. As in the story by Cisneros that I began with, Spanish is the language of their childhood. The mother begins with nostalgic flashbacks to the past, which is captured in her recreation of their little voices in the phrase *"Vamos a pedirle dulces a mamá. Vamos."* These reflections end with the words "But that was in Mexico," and form a sharp contrast with the present: "But now my children go to American high schools." The poem is a psychological portrait of Elena's separation and disconnection from her family, of her embarrassment at not functioning linguistically in the new society, and her humiliation as she locks herself in the bathroom to, "say the thick words softly, for if I stop trying, I will be deaf/ when my children need my help."

"Unnatural Speech" (*Borders* 17–18) represents a second psychological portrait and metalinguistic reflection on language and linguistic dominance. The poem explores the psychological effects of adapting to the dominant language. Here a Mexican American C.P.A. reflects on her voicelessness and fear of blundering when speaking English. As a bicultural individual, she is schizophrenic—a typical condition, according to Alica Gaspar de Alba, for many Chicanas.[12] Her fractured identity finds expression in her use of "you" vs. "I". The "I," or the speaker's U.S.-American self, takes on the voice of authority and states provocatively "my English language scares / you"; she takes a detached look at the shy and unconfident "you" and reminds her how she used to practice speeches for school in front of her dolls, and still

> Now at twenty
> you stand before
> those dolls tense,
> feet together,
> tongue thick, dry,
> pushing heavy English
> words out.

Contrasted with this difficulty is the speaker's ease in singing in Spanish: "*Víbora, víbora de la mar*"; now the words are "light" in her mouth. The sea serpent here becomes the metaphor for English, and it is these vipers, the speaker suggests, that the "you" needs to learn how to hold at bay.

Mora's strategic placement of a single Spanish line in an English-dominant poem can have tremendous effects. In the second group of poems it has the effect of allowing readers to see the separation of cultures in the borderlands. The poetic parody "Bilingual Christmas" (*Borders* 21) mocks the perfunctory use of Spanish—the few phrases that have taken hold in American consciousness, phrases that through their wide dissemination in popular culture need no translation. The poem echoes Spanish phrases like "*Buenos días*," "*hasta luego*", "*feliz navidad*," and "*próspero año nuevo*," but it also mocks snippets of English songs and begins with the call "*Do you hear what I hear?*" which triggers two different responses based on divergent perspectives. While the *mexicanos* are spatially united with European Americans in this poem's setting, a company's board room, the poem's structure enacts division as the chair person's comments are printed in a broad column on the left side of the page, and the Mexican Americans' answers in a slim one on the right side.[13] As the poem develops, it becomes clear that the reality the "I" of the traditional Christmas song hears and sees is not at all what the Mexican

American Other/marginalized border person experiences. The poem ironically represents the voice of the white speaker, "Where are your grateful holiday smiles, / bilinguals? I've given you a voice, / let you in." These words mock the patronizing attitude of opening up boardrooms for the entrance of a few token Chicanos/as who are invited to join the club. In blunt contrast to the chair's jocular tone is the bilinguals' serious answer:

> Not carols we hear
> whimpering
> children too cold
> to sing
> on Christmas eve.

The second stanza repeats, with a difference, the song's initial call, "Do you see what I see," to which the chair responds with yet another comment about his generosity, "adding a dash of color to conferences and corporate parties / one per panel or office / slight South-of-the-border seasoning." This is again contrasted with the view of the Mexican American "exotic" Other:

> Not twinkling lights
> we see but
> search lights
> seeking illegal aliens
> outside our thick windows.

Through its construction and its message "Bilingual Christmas" illustrates the clash of cultures, placing them in a dialogue with each other, and questioning a unitary world view. The poem undermines official cultural discourses of pluralism, integration, and diversity through parody.

However, the use of Spanish has a different effect when the language is strategically seized and reclaimed by bilinguals. It can then become a tactic of empowerment. The last poem of Mora's collection *Chants* (1984) is indicative of this strategy. In "Legal Alien" (60) Mora writes,

> Bi-lingual, Bi-cultural,
> able to slip from "How's life?"
> To "*Me'stan volviendo loca.*"

Mora's use of Spanish in the third line of the poem (again, the only Spanish in the poem) is, from a postmodern perspective, a play with language that experimentally transgresses the boundaries between two very different linguistic systems. This form of linguistic transgression thus does not position English and Spanish at opposite ends of a spectrum but creates a third term, a new mestiza language, made up of components of both. It is the language of the bicultural individual, someone who is neither American nor Mexican but both:

American but hyphenated,
viewed by Anglos as perhaps exotic,
perhaps inferior, definitely different,
viewed by Mexicans as alien, . . .
An American to Mexicans,
a Mexican to Americans.

It is a language that fosters healing by forming a group consciousness, where not everyone will understand that "they're driving me crazy." The line shows the bicultural speaker's command of both languages; despite her "token" status, this speaker, like many Mexican Americans, is "able" to slip easily from English to Spanish.

Spanish in "La Migra" *(Agua Santa* 104–5) is also portrayed as a secret and liberating code, a language that is unintelligible to non-bilingual speakers, and one that helps perform a reversal of power relations. "La Migra" enacts and simultaneously deconstructs a bifurcation in its two stanzas, each of which relates a short monologue spoken by playing children: "Let's play La Migra" (104), both stanzas begin. But whereas in the first one the child claims the authoritative role of the border patrol officer and assigns the role of Mexican maid to her or his playmate, in the second one the roles are reversed. In the first version, the agent in his shiny new Jeep captures and handcuffs the maid, but in the second one the patrol agent is stranded in the desert while the Mexican woman knows how to navigate the territory; she remarks, "all you have is heavy: hat, / glasses, badge, shoes, gun." In contrast, she says "I know this desert / where to rest, / where to drink." The poem's only Spanish line is inserted into the text without the traditional italics that would mark its difference, suggesting the "maid's" degree of comfort in both languages. The words "Agua dulce brota aquí, aquí, aquí" contain information crucial for survival in the desert, and are symptomatic of a reversal of traditional hierarchies. While in the first stanza the "officer" asserts his power by telling the "maid" to be silent, "I can take you wherever / I want, but don't ask questions because / I don't speak Spanish," the poem undermines his claims to power and self-reflexively stresses the advantage of bilingualism in its conclusion:

"but since you can't speak Spanish,/ you do not understand," simultaneously mocking and displacing the authority figure.

Since 1848, Bruce-Novoa explains, speaking Spanish could be seen as a political act. While interlingual poetry is clearly experimental and innovative, and, one might add, postmodern, it certainly forces readers to consider the context of the colonization of the Spanish language in the southwestern United States and the effects that colonization has had on individuals and their cultures. Mora's writing highlights the role of language—language's potential to divide and connect, to empower and disenfranchize. Her recuperation of Spanish shows interlingualism clearly not as a deficit but as a strategic act of defiance, as a gesture of validation, and of questioning worldviews. In her combination of Spanish and English, Mora creates cultural *mestizaje*—a concept that, in Anzaldúa's formulation, inherently implies revision. In her essay "How to Tame a Wild Tongue," Anzaldúa asks,

> For a people who are neither Spanish nor live in a country in which Spanish is the first language; for a people who live in a country in which English is the reigning tongue but who are not Anglos; for a people who cannot entirely identify with either standard (formal, Castillian) Spanish nor standard English, what recourse is left to them but to create their own language? . . . We speak a patois, a forked tongue, a variation of two languages. (*Borderlands* 55)

She claims that language as the territory, the homeland of the mestiza and says, "We are your linguistic nightmare, your linguistic aberration, your linguistic *mestisaje* [sic], the subject of your *burla*" (*Borderlands* 58).

To counter historical dividing lines, Pat Mora explains in her essay collection *Nepantla,* the poet can intervene by building bridges, initiating dialogues, and fostering communication:

> the Chicana writer seeks to *heal* cultural wounds of historical neglect by providing opportunities to remember the past, to *share* and *ease* bitterness, to describe what has been viewed as unworthy of description, to *cure* by incantations and rhythms, by listening with her entire being and responding. She then gathers the tales and myths, weaves them together, and, if lucky, casts spells. (131; emphasis added)

For Mora, as for poet Adrienne Rich, contemporary poetry comes out of what Rich called the "points of stress" in a society, or, as Mora puts it here, "cultural wounds of historical neglect." As a poet, Mora sees herself not as some other Chicana poets do, as a *bruja*, a witch, one who "knows eerie secrets and who can manipulate words as she gazes at the world with frightening eyes" (125), but instead as a *curandera* (a faith healer), an oral communicator who uses "a gentler power" (125). The poet/*curandera* "creates an informal atmosphere conducive to holistic healing—healing of affirmation, identification, confirmation, wholeness" (128), and she "manipulates the symbols that are part of her patients' experience base to ease communication" (131). Mora's latest collection of poetry, entitled *Agua Santa, Holy Water*, echoes the healing aspects of poetry and storytelling through its extensive use of water symbolism and of ritualistic images of cleansing and healing.

Conclusion:
Decolonizing the Postmodern

In looking at this book that I'm almost finished writing, I see a mosaic pattern (Aztec-like) emerging, a weaving pattern, thick here, thick there. . . . I see the barely contained color threatening to spill over the boundaries of the object it represents and into other "objects" and over the borders of the frame. I see a hybridzation of metaphor, different species of ideas popping up here, popping up there, full of variations and seeming contradictions, though I believe in an ordered, structured universe where all phenomena are interrelated and imbued with spirit. This almost finished product seems an assemblage, a central core, now appearing, now disappearing in a crazy dance.

Gloria Anzalúa, *Borderlands* (66)

In her essay "The Alter-Native Grain: Theorizing Chicano/a Popular Culture," Alicia Gaspar de Alba ruminates on the conceptions of "theory" that "exclude . . . the popular and the marginalized" (103). Theory today, she argues "is privileged contemplation engaged in by those who have the leisure to pursue speculation beyond need" (103). She continues, "As historical objects of that vision, women, people of color, the working classes, and oral traditions have all been *overlooked* by theory" (103). Theories, then, and postmodern/poststructuralist theories are no exception, have participated in the same processes of colonization in the cultural realm that have worked to marginalize Chicanas in other social, cultural, and political institutions. Hegemonic claims of postmodern theories, such as their narrow focus on textual experimentation, have had the effect of both denying Chicana authors into the pantheon of postmodern artists, and of overlooking their contributions to (postmodern) theorizing. "What is considered theory in the dominant academic community is not necessarily what counts as theory for women-of-color," Anzaldúa writes ("Haciendo caras" xxv), and she adds, "we need to de-academize theory and to connect the community to the academy" (xxvi).

Chicana authors and critics *have* been connecting the community to the academy precisely by producing such texts as Anzaldúa describes in the above epigraph *and* by highlighting the theoretical implications of such texts. They have produced texts whose weaving pattern reveals a multi-layered art and whose spill-over of boundaries questions stable categories. Woven together are the varieties of language, cultural practices, and epistemological systems that coexist in the borderlands. Code-switching, the incorporation of folkloric elements such as folktales, legends, or remedios, and the inclusion of popular genres such as *telenovelas* result in a variety of syncretic formations and a hybridity that constitutes the particular contribution of Chicanas to the contemporary critique of modernity. Beyond stylistic innovation, these vernacular forms instead raise broader issues regarding language and its functioning, history and its writing, and knowledge and its achievement. About the resulting polyphonous and multivocal texts, Anzaldúa suggests: "our strength lies in shifting perspectives" ("Haciendo caras" xxvii). These shifting perspectives clearly derive from specific bicultural experiences and are hence related to conditions of postcoloniality. As Américo Paredes suggests, the border "is not simply a line on a map but, more fundamentally . . . a sensitized area where two cultures or two political systems come face to face" (qtd. in Rouse 15). In this sensitized area, textual production is political, as it is aesthetic and theoretical. Again in the words of Anzaldúa: "creative acts are forms of political activism employing definite aesthetic strategies for resisting dominant cultural norms and are not merely aesthetic exercises" ("Haciendo caras" xxiv).

With respect to the relationship between postmodernism and Latin American art, Pedro Lange-Churión and Eduardo Mendieta make the following case:

> The onus . . . is not on showing whether Latin America is postmodern, but on how a certain path to and through (Post)modernity is Latin American; more precisely, how certain (Post)modernity is very Latin American. Culturally, economically, and politically many Latin American countries have struggled with the issues of the heterogeneity of the "cultural" realm, the hybridization of "high" culture by so-called low culture, the permeation of the political by the economic and the over-determination of both by "cultural" icons and ideologies that have been products as much of colonial traditions, as of neocolonialism, nationalism, and the striving after democratic self-determination. (27)

In analogy, I have argued that Chicanas have forged "a path to and through (Post)modernity." Theirs is a variety of postmodernism that has nonetheless, and through its politics, nudged postmodern theories in new directions. Postmodernism today, through the contributions of Chicanas, women, and other minority artists, is much less monolithic, and postmodern theorizing has become a much more rigorous engagement with postmodernity.

If, as Lange-Churión and Mendieta argue, "(Post)modernity is the crisis and abandonment of the pursuits after the unity of reason, selves, societies, and history" (20), then Chicana cultural production has not only been an integral part of postmodernity but has also participated in a critical examination of postmodernism's Euro-centric biases.[1] Chicana writing is part of the process of decolonizing the postmodern.

Notes

Introduction: Toward a Chicana Postmodernism

1. For histories of the Chicano movement, see Matt S. Meier and Feliciano Rivera's *Mexican Americans, American Mexicans*, as well as Ignacio García's *Chicanismo*.

2. For more extended discussions of the relationship between Chicanos and Chicanas than is possible here, see Alma M. García and Angie Chabram-Dernersesian ("I Throw Punches"). See also Paula M.L. Moya for a helpful summary of Chicanas' reaction to the movement.

3. See A.M. García 4–7.

4. See Chabram-Dernersesian on revisionist imagery of the Virgen by artists such as Yolanda López and Ester Hernández ("I Throw Punches"). For important discussions of Chicana revisions of La llorona, see Saldívar-Hull (*Feminism*), José E. Limón ("La llorona"), Norma Alarcón ("Traddutora"), and also Viramontes's short story, "Tears on My Pillow." Literary artists such as Carmen Tafolla, Angela de Hoyos, and Margarita Cota-Cárdenas, among others, offer contemporary portrayals of Malinche. See also Sonia Saldívar-Hull's personal account of how Chicana poetry such as de Hoyos's helped shape her consciousness by exposing the internal contradictions of the movement *(Feminism* 12-26).

5. See also Ihab Hassan, especially his "Toward a Concept of Postmodernism," for a page-long list of strategies that distinguish postmodernism from modernism (91–2).

6. See also Peter Bürger's discussion of the form-content dichotomy in avant-garde art.

7. In *The Order of Things*, Michel Foucault establishes an "episteme" as the regime of truth, the arrangement of knowledges that characterizes all of the discourses of a particular period. See also Nelly Richard for a valuable discussion of modernity/postmodernity in a Latin American context.

8. See also the more recent publication by McHale, *Constructing Postmodernism* (1992), which still adheres to a formalist paradigm of the postmodern.

9. See also the studies published in the 1990s by Ellen McCracken and Raúl Homero Villa.

10. In his "Theories of the Postmodern," Jameson, in structuralist fashion, creates a symmetrical model to illustrate positions on postmodernism: critics are divided into the anti-modernist and pro-postmodern or anti-modernist and anti-postmodernist camps, or they are pro-modernist and pro-postmodernist, or pro-modernist anti-postmodernists (61).

11. This is a common motif: Sonia Saldívar-Hull also says that postmodernism beyond the aesthetic has not been sufficiently theorized *(Feminism* 85–6). José Davíd Saldívar rejects mainstream postmodernism's art-culture system *(Border* 9).

12. For useful critiques of the nostalgia for the unitary subject on the part of what Gayatri Chakravorty Spivak calls "hegemonic feminism," specifically in feminist standpoint epistemology, see Alarcón ("The Theoretical Subject(s)" 357); Grewal (233); and Angela McRobbie, who asks "which social subjects have had the privilege of being whole, or 'healthy', and thus fully inscribed in history and in culture? . . . To lament the decline of full wholesome subjectivity is literally to cast aspersions on unwholesome, un(in)formed, partial and hybridic identities" (4). See also Nancy K. Miller's response to proclamations of the Death of the author: "women have not had the same historical relation of identity to origin, institution, production, that men have had, women have not, I think, (collectively) felt burdened by too much Self, Ego, Cogito" (106).

13. Sinologist Rey Chow also presents a convincing critical response to postmodernism as "global culture." She takes as her occasion Jameson's observation of the postmodern nature of Taiwanese writer Wang Wenxing's work and exposes such universalizing as ethnocentric and monological, questioning the translatability of Euro-American periodizing concepts such as modernism and postmodernism into a different cultural context.

14. One might argue that a similar critique is possible with respect to Marxism. How do its Euro-centric roots aid or hinder its translation into a Latin American context?

15. See also Marta Ester Sánchez, who reads postmodernism as a movement that has been enabling for Chicana poetic expression (18); Cordelia Candelaria, who employs the Derridean concept of *différance* in her analysis of the novel *Bless Me Ultima* and other ethnic texts. According to Candelaria, postmodernism's usefulness resides in its "iconoclastic and subversive" nature. She continues, "By positioning itself outside the credo of one real reality, one true philosophy, and an inelastic language of referentiality, deconstruction theory lends literary criticism an expressive calculus that is not dependent on a shared ideology or metaphysics as a precondition to its application" (191); Gloria Anzaldúa, who, in an interview with Andrea Lunsford, acknowledges intersections with poststructural theory but insists on her own different naming of common principles and on the primacy of the indigenous in her work (64–5); and Norma Alarcón, who recognizes postmodernism's usefulness in undermining the hegemony of liberal feminism ("Theoretical Subjects" 127).

16. See also Pat Mora's *Nepantla* for similar generic hybridization.

17. Elsewhere, Gaspar de Alba defines schizophrenia as "the presence of mutually contradictory or antagonistic beliefs, social forms, and material traits in any group whose racial, religious, or social components are a hybrid (or *mestizaje*) of two or more fundamentally opposite cultures," and she continues, "I argue that the awareness of cultural schizophrenia is fundamental to the evolution of Chicano/a consciousness because that awareness leads to identity crisis, to rupture between the outwardly-defined persona (or the colonized mind) and the inwardly-identified self" ("The Alter-Native Grain" 106; 107).

18. For similar revisitations of marginal locations, see Homi Bhabha, Mary Louise Pratt (*Imperial Eyes*), and Paul Jay. Sandoval and Pérez (*Decolonial Imaginary*) most explicitly link marginal locations such as third space feminism with postmodernism.

19. Richard similarly comments on the potential of postmodernism to foreground the previously unspoken: "By creating the possibility of a critical re-reading of modernity, postmodernism offers us the chance to reconsider all that was 'left unsaid' and to inject its areas of opacity and resistance with the potential for new, as yet undiscovered, meanings" (12).

20. See also Stephen Connor for such a critique of postmodern discourses.

21. See also Grewal and Kaplan ("Introduction") and Richard (10) for suggestingg that the multiple and hybrid past of Latin American and Chicano/a experiences render these experiences and literary expressions as postmodern *avant la lettre*.

Chapter 1
Narratives of the Border: Postmodern Hybridity, Barbed Wire Fences, and **Mestizaje**

1. See also Caren Kaplan's discussion of the significance of the language of geography in cultural studies ("Reconfigurations" 25).

2. For the prominence of the border in the Chicano/a imaginary, see José David Saldívar *(Border Matters)* and Debra A. Castillo and María Socorro Tabuenca Córdoba, as well as Louis Mendoza, who all discuss various textualizations of this concept.

3. In his interview with Henri Ronse, Derrida explains that each of his books is subject to the same overrun of borders: "One can take *Of Grammatology* as a long essay articulated in two parts . . . *into the middle* of which one could staple *Writing and Difference*" *(Positions* 4). See also *Positions* 13–14 for a return to this idea.

4. Derrida takes issue with this "normative" position in "The Law of Genre." See chapter four of this study.

5. See, for example, Mae Henderson's collection of essays in *Borders, Boundaries, and Frames* (1995); Elizabeth A. Meese's study *Crossing the Double-Cross. The Practice of Feminist Criticism* (1986); or Margaret R. Higonnet's *Borderwork: Feminist Engagements with Comparative Literature (1994).* Though the essays Henderson has collected participate in the postmodern deconstruction of borders, Henderson also draws attention to the perils of literal border crossings (2). She writes, "In metaphoring notions of border and borderlands, we must keep in mind 'what losses of specificity—of class, power, and histories of oppression—[such a] transposition [might] entail' . . . In the geopolitical context, colonized peoples frequently suffer border incursions that carry with them violent intent to colonize" (26). Overall, however, the essays in this volume view border crossing as an "act of creation rather than one of violation" (26).

6. As a result of the Schengen Agreement between European Union countries (June 1990), by 1995 checks had completely been abolished at the borders between Germany, France, Belgium, the Netherlands, Luxembourg, Austria, Italy, Spain, Portugal, and Greece.

7. This backlash is by no means exclusive to the U.S. Issues of immigration were on the front burner in the 1998 German elections. The conservative coalition led by then Chancellor Helmut Kohl supported limiting the number of immigrants and demanded a greater willingness on the part of foreigners to integrate into German society, ideas that have since been adopted by the current coalition led by Gerhard Schröder. The nationalist backlash manifests itself in the rhetoric of the opposition Christian Democratic party, which calls for adherence to a German *Leitkultur* (guiding culture) based on Christian and Enlightenment values. It also informs politics elsewhere in Europe, as for instance in Austrian Jörg Haider's offensives against *Überfremdung* (over-foreignization), Berlusconi-led Italy's defense of the nation state, or Denmark's recent resolutions against immigration.

8. One possible reading of government officials' idea of making the border wall/fence open and friendly is that it reflects the modern state's ingenuity in co-opting the postmodern rhetoric of permeable borders for its ideological purposes. I would like to thank Marianne DeKoven for pointing

this out to me.

9. For an in-depth study of the gradual militarization of the border, see Timothy J. Dunn's *The Militarization of the U.S.-Mexico Border 1978–1992*. Dunn applies the military doctrine of Low Intensity Conflict, developed during the 1980s to counter perceived threats to national security particularly from regions in Central America, to the U.S.-Mexico border area. The policy's goal is the "maintenance of social control over targeted civilian populations" through implementation of military measures (4).

10. See also Dunn for a discussion of this incompatibility (117–122). To critics of military deployment along the border, these common efforts further raise legal issues, since it violates the 1878 Posse Comitatus law, which forbids U.S. military from engaging in domestic police work.

11. Much of the hardware frenzy seems to derive from lawmakers responding to business lobbies rather than from the Border Patrol itself. The House threatened to withhold new funds if the agency does not try out new Unmanned Aerial Vehicles (UAVs) formerly used in the Gulf War and in Bosnia for surveillance. The chief of Air Operations for the Border Patrol commented that manufacturers "regularly pitch their latest border surveillance products" (O'Connell, "Lawmakers" B4).

12. For discussions of the border in Chicano/a discourse, see, for instance, Mario T. García's "*La Frontera*: The Border as Symbol and Reality in Mexican American Thought;" much of Guillermo Gómez-Peña's work, including "Documented/Undocumented;" Emily D. Hicks's book-length study *Border Writing: The Multidimensional Text*; Renato Rosaldo's "Politics, Patriarchs, and Laughter;" Sonia Saldívar-Hull's *Feminism on the Border* (176, note 1, where she claims that Anzaldúa's text marks the beginning of a "cottage industry of border writing"); and José David Saldívar's "The Limits of Cultural Studies" and particularly *Border Matters: Remapping American Cultural Studies*.

13. Derrida's comment on the relationship between upper and lower band in "BORDER LINES" provides an interesting parallel to Anzaldúa's prose and poetry sections: the upper band (the longer essay) is characterized by "semantic accumulation and overloading," the lower by "economy and formalization" (90–91). See also Jane Hedley's claim that repetition and recapitulation are the hallmark of Anzaldúa's mythographic approach (46).

14. For discussions of Anzaldúa's generic boundary crossings see Diane P. Freedman, *An Alchemy of Genres*, especially 31–65; Kate Adams, "North American Silences;" and Saldívar-Hull's "Feminism on the Border."

15. For a discussion of the mestiza and Coatlicue, see for instance Yvonne Yarbro-Bejarano's excellent article "Gloria Anzaldúa's *Borderlands/La frontera*: Cultural Studies, 'Difference,' and the Non-Unitary Subject;" Jane Hedley's "Nepantilist Poetics: Narrative and Cultural Identity in the Mixed-Language Writings of Irena Klepfisz and Gloria Anzaldúa;" María Lugones's "On *Borderlands/La Frontera*: an Interpretive Essay.*"

16. Diane L. Fowlkes, writing about Anzaldúa's work, points out the resemblance between borders and Cartesian categories "in that they require a person to be one place or another exclusively" (115). Borderland studies, in contrast, stress that one can be both/and.

17. Ellwyn R. Stoddard stresses this artificiality: "Residents all along the U.S.-Mexican border have in their backyards that federal installation called a national border over which they have little control and which *capriciously* divides cities, institutions, families, and countries" (4; emphasis added).

18. Translations are all mine.

Chapter 2
Performing Identities: Spatial Metaphors and Subjectivity in Anzaldúa, Mora, and Viramontes

1. See, for instance, historian Emma Pérez, who locates Chicana history in the interstitial gaps: "It is in such locations that oppositional, subaltern histories can be found" (5), she says.

2. For Chicana theorizations of multiple subjectivity, see Norma Alarcón's critique of Anglo-American standpoint theory and of the self-sufficient and individualist subject of mainstream feminism ("Theoretical Subjects" 357), and Angie Chabram-Dernersesian's critique of the Chicano movement's collective (male) subject ("I Throw Punches").

3. Kaplan further argues that radical as they may seem, these postmodern/poststructuralist tropes actually reveal many continuities with modernist theories of dislocation, specifically those of exile and expatriation. Modernist exile became an *aesthetic* category, and the modernist metropolis fostered creativity.

4. See Rafael Pérez-Torres, *Movements in Chicano Poetry,* on Chicano/a literary depictions of migrants and nomads (especially chapter four). See also Chandra Talpade Mohanty who states that "movement *between* cultures, languages, and complex configurations of meaning and power have always been the territory of the colonized" (Mohanty, "Feminist Encounters" 42). Similarly, Michelle Wallace claims, "the post-modern critique mirrors the outsider's or the migrant's or the nomad's sense of being in the world" (53).

5. See also Kaplan, who argues that identities are formed through the mediating activities of places, locations, and positions (*Questions* 185).

6. For related discussions, see Kaplan, who argues that "postmodern theories that link subject positions to geological and metaphorical locations have emerged out of a perception that periodization and linear historical forms of explanation have been unable to account fully for the production of complex identities in an era of diaspora and displacement." But she also issues a warning— "Yet, any exclusive recourse to space, place, or position becomes utterly abstract and universalizing without historical specificity." She therefore calls for "a critical practice that deconstructs standard historical periodization and demystifies abstract spatial metaphors" ("The Politics" 138). Much of this demystification is indebted to Michel Foucault, who proclaimed, "Space is fundamental in any form of communal life; space is fundamental in any exercise of power" (252). Robert Carr underscores the necessity of connecting space to history: "Narratives of geography are at stake in narratives of history, and vice versa, as both are caught up in the imperialist agenda of remapping the world" (154). In his "topospatial readings," José David Saldívar's goal "is to show profound interaction of space and history, geography and psychology, nationhood and imperialism, and to define space as not just a 'setting' but as a formative presence throughout" (*Border Matters* 79). Perhaps most pertinently, Raúl Homero Villa identifies three subordinating practices that define Chicano social space: "(1) the physical regulation and constitution of space (via land-use decisions and the built environment); (2) the social control of space (via legal/juridical state apparatuses and police authority); and (3) the ideological control of space (via the interpellation of citizen-subjects through educational and informational apparatuses)" (3–4).

7. Tey Diana Rebolledo also contrasts Anglo and Mexican American inscriptions of the land. Her discussion focuses on the rewriting of the landscape by Anglo settlers who saw the land "without traditions and roots, a land representing primal freedom" ("Tradition" 96).

8. The borderlands are thus not exclusively the territory of Mexican Americans. Arlene R. Keizer, for example, has related the concept to West Africans encountering slavery in the U.S. She explains "sites at which these two systems come into conflict are the sites at which black identities are formed, maintained, and transformed" (106).

9. See also Biddy Martin and Chandra Talpade Mohanty's critique of home in their reading of Pratt's text. They similarly observe that "lesbianism . . . makes 'home' impossible" (202).

10. For another example of writers' creations of such heterotopias, Foucauldian oppositional spaces, see Melvin Dixon, who argues that African American writers use the trope of the underground as a transitional space of self-creation (5) in an overall attempt to counter dislocation and alienation, and to create alternative landscapes where black culture and identity can flourish.

11. For other critiques of this appropriation, see Pérez-Torres ("Chicano Ethnicity" 169) and Alarcón ("Conjugating" 129–32).

12. The preponderance of psychological terminology, and especially of "schizophrenia" in discussions of Chicana identity provides another link to poststructuralist theory. Thus Deleuze and Guattari link schizophrenia to deterritorialization. Schizophrenia is central to Fredric Jameson's definition of postmodern culture ("Postmodernism"). Anzaldúa speaks of "mental nepantilism" (*Borderlands* 78). For other Chicana uses of this link, see Alicia Gaspar de Alba ("Literary" 291) or La Chrisx (84). This discourse is, however, not confined to Chicanas and poststructuralists. Caribbean poet Michelle Wallace explains, "my process, or my location, is necessarily schizophrenic and dialogical in that it originates from multiple positions which are not my own, which cannot be reconciled or contained by one another . . . I did not know then that I needed to insist on occupying these and more locations simultaneously" (50–1). She continues, "To be 'black' is to be 'crazy' . . . a nomadic process, not a location but multiple locations, not a homeland but a temporary and provisional resting place" (52).

13. For critical assessments of the politics of location and the impact of this concept on contemporary feminisms, see Kaplan ("The Politics"), Friedman, Wallace, and bell hooks.

Chapter 3
"True Fictions": Norma Elía Cantú's Strategic Realism

1. For photography as a form of writing, see Alan Trachtenberg, Walter Benn Michaels, and Susan Sontag. Trachtenberg applauds James E. McClees's choice of the term "writing with light" for the new art because it places photography among familiar practices of constructing meaning, such as writing and drawing (3–4).

2. See Sontag, who argues that photography teaches us a new visual code (3).

3. In his essay "Ethnicity and the Post-Modern Arts of Memory," Michael M.J. Fischer suggests that this self-reflexivity is characteristic of many ethnic autobiographies (232).

4. I chose the term "strategic realism" in analogy to Spivak's "strategic essentialism." In her discussion of subaltern studies Spivak endorses disenfranchized people's strategic employment of foundationalist views (205). Diana Fuss presents a similar argument in her insightful reexamination of "essentialism," often used as a hostile epithet in feminist circles. She negotiates between constructivist and essentialist (ie. biologist or foundationalist) views and argues for a strategic use of essentialism while showing awareness of its limitations.

5. Note that in Linda Hutcheon's view, this is a typically postmodern move. A "use and abuse of conventions" is characteristic of postmodern artists. Hutcheon elaborates, "postmodernism is a contradictory phenomenon, one that uses and abuses, installs and then subverts, the very concepts it challenges" (*Poetics* 3).

6. Fisher has noted the common intersection in ethnic autobiographies of the individual and the social. He states that "what thus seem initially to be individualistic autobiographical searchings turn out to be revelations of traditions" (198).

7. Clifford's elaboration concerning his use of the term "fiction" is useful both for an understanding of the projects of ethnography and autobiography: drawing on recent textual theories' recuperation of the term from its connotations of falsehood and untruth, he argues that viewing ethnography as fiction highlights rather something made or fashioned, and he concludes, "good ethnographies [are] 'true fictions'" ("Introduction" 6).

8. Among the essays that best make this point are Mary Louise Pratt's, who in her exploration of the tension between the personal and the ethnographic "scientific" narrative, identifies tropes that tend to mystify the ethnographer's position ("Fieldwork"); Vincent Crapanzano's, who explains how ethnographic events are often sacrificed to rhetorical functions of literary discourse—a transcendental vision writers want to put forth; Renato Rosaldo's, who discusses the ethnographers' longing for a transhuman pastoralism that guides their search and their writing ("From the Door"); and Clifford's own, in which he shows how supposedly realistic portraits are more often than not allegorical ("On Ethnographic").

9. See also Roland Barthes, who, in his desire to distinguish photography from historiography envisions the former as a realistic discourse, the latter as a relativistic one: Words, even the most realistic attempts at discourse as in historiography, he argues, frequently point to imaginary referents, to "chimeras" (76), mediating reality without accurately reflecting it. Historiography is "a memory fabricated" (93) without grounding in truth.

10. Barthes's self-professed realism may surprise readers used to thinking of Barthes as a poststructuralist critic at the end of his career when, after all, *Camera Lucida* was written. Indeed, it is a contested and often contradictory book. Thus his idea of portrait photography seems to undermine his claims to realism. When he suggests that individual poses transform the person into an image, he sounds more like Pierre Bourdieu than Roland Barthes; moreover, the idea of "camera lucida", the projection of a virtual image, challenges his claims. See also John Tagg, who explains Barthes's position by suggesting that Barthes's book was born out of his nostalgia for the passing of his mother, "which produces in him a longing for a pre-linguistic certainty and unity—a regressive phantasy" (4). The persistence of a photographic rhetoric of authority and certainty is moreover evident in the works of recent critics examining the intersections of life writing and photography, who argue with Barthes that photography provides the certainty that words cannot. Hence Carol E. Neubauer reads Maxine Hong Kingston's use of the family album as an authentication device, as juxtaposed to the unreliability of memory. Similarly, Betty Bergland uses the rhetoric of photographic evidence as necessary for immigrant narratives, such as Mary Antin's *The Promised Land*.

11. For a very different assessment of family photography, see Pierre Bourdieu, who argues against the notion that this activity, "which has no traditions and makes no demands, would be delivered over to the anarchy of individual improvisation, it appears that there is nothing more regulated and conventional than photographic practice and amateur photographs" (7). He later suggests that "There are few activities which are so stereotyped and less abandoned to the anarchy of individual intentions" (19).

12. See Sontag, who also argues that photographs *confer* importance (28).

13. See York on de Man's theory of photography's de-contextualization.

14. While Bourdieu states that family photography is part of the cult of the domestic (19), Susan Sontag points out the irony in the family's desire to chronicle itself in an age when the very notion of family is being contested.

15. For Bakhtin's outline of the process of ideological identity formation, see his section "The Speaking Person in the Novel" (*Dialogic Imagination* 331–66).

16. For Walter Benjamin, *memento mori,* the remembrance of loved ones, constitutes the "cult value" of the photograph (226).

17. For early written ethnographies of Mexican Americans in South Texas by John Gregory Bourke, Frank Dobie, and Jovita Gonzales, see Limón (*Dancing*) and José David Saldívar (*Border Matters*). Significantly, Bourke entitled one essay about the Rio Grande Valley "The American Congo" (Saldívar 164).

18. See Coco Fusco's excellent discussion of Mexican photography, in which she argues that Mexican photographers, in their attempts to capture *mexicanidad*, rely on a similar inventory of images of Mexicans as peasants, "rural, timeless, and brimming with natural beauty and supernatural belief" (105). Mexican images of Mexicanness, she argues, dovetail perfectly with American images of the Other. For a depiction of Mexican Americans that is very different from the FSA-commissioned images, see Thomas H. Kreneck's *Del Pueblo: A Pictoral History of the Houston Hispanic Community*. Kreneck collected pictures from community members themselves, and the book reflects an urban scene full of organizations: self-help groups, political action groups, church organizations, women's clubs, musical clubs, etc.

19. See also Montejano, who explains that Texas independence and the annexation of northern Mexican territory were regarded as reflections of a "manifest destiny," a victory of the Anglo Saxon nation over an inferior Indian race (24).

Chapter 4
Little Women *Meets* **The Flintstones***: Mixing Genres and Blending Cultures in Ana Castillo's* **So Far From God** *and Sandra Cisneros's "Little Miracles, Kept Promises"*

1. One of the targets of Derrida's discussion here, one might note, is Gerard Genette, whose insistence, in structuralist fashion, on keeping distinct classifications, particularly those of genre and mode, is the object of Derrida's derision.

2. While this chapter specifically examines the novel's relation to the family saga and the *telenovela*, the palimpsestic nature of the text evokes multiple intertexts. Folkloric elements such as *remedios* and recipes in Castillo's novel recall a tradition of *nuevo mexicana* writers, specifically Fabiola Cabeza de Baca Gilbert's *The Good Life: New Mexico Traditions and Food* (1949), which combines creative tales about a mythic family living in an isolated village in New Mexico with recipes for the preparation of traditional foods. Parallels to this text deserve a more extended discussion than is possible here. Most obviously, Castillo evokes early Christian legends that turned the Greek goddess Sofia and her daughters into martyrs (Saeta "An Interview" 21 and "A *MELUS* Interview" 146–7). Mary Ann Bernal elaborates on the parallel of Fe, Esperanza, and Caridad (Faith, Hope, and Charity), three saints who were venerated in the early Christian Church for their reported martyrdom in Rome under Hadrian (24).

3. For discussions of the reproduction of values in family sagas, see Lori Ween, Maria Roof, Martin B. Swales, and Christine Bridgewood.

4. See Marta Ester Sánchez for a discussion of traditions of community activism among Mexican American women (6) and also Rebolledo and Rivero for an overview of traditional images of the "Chile queen" (saloon woman) or the enduring, self-sacrificing mother (1). Moreover, Elsa Saeta's interviews with Ana Castillo shed some light on the evolution of Sofi's activism in previous drafts of the novel, which originated in the short story "Loca Santa" ("An Interview" 19). In one version Sofi, in analogy to early Christian mythology, ends up crying on the grave of her three martyred daughters. Castillo comments: "But my agent who was reading the manuscript commented that 'Well, this is very depressing. You know, you promised Norton a happy ending.' So I thought, 'what would she [Sofi] do to change that, particularly as a religious figure. What would she do?' She takes over, she doesn't submit to that point in history when patriarchy took over her authority" ("An Interview" 21 and "A *MELUS* Interview" 147).

5. De Lauretis has pointed out that in the postmodern age, effective resistance can occur on a local rather than global level: "With respect to gender, new constructions can be posed . . . in the micropolitical practices of daily life and daily resistances that afford both agency and sources of power" (*Technologies* 24). See also Eliana Ortega and Nancy Saporta Sternbach for a discussion of politics from the kitchen table as a characteristic of Latina literature (17).

6. Other parallels and points of departure are Beth's prolonged and saintly death, which provides a foil for Loca's death and veneration as a saint at the end of Castillo's novel. While Beth's character is firmly rooted in a Victorian context of True Womanhood, ironically Loca, despite her lack of contact with people, dies of AIDS. Another point of departure is that *So Far From God* depicts women's lives beyond and outside of marriage. Only Fe gets married for reasons of propriety, and all the daughters die within rapid succession.

7. In fact, the names of the novel's characters recall a Mexican *telenovela* "Fe, Esperanza y Caridad" with allegorically named characters representing socially sanctioned feminine virtues. Caridad always helps the poor in church, while Castillo's Caridad shows charity as a curandera; Fe leads a very religious life, while ironically, materialism is the religion of Castillo's Fe; and Esperanza's optimism parallels the political activism of Castillo's Esperanza. I would like to thank Liliana Castañeda-Rossmann for pointing out these parallels.

8. In an interview with NPR's Noah Adams, Castillo vouches for the plausibility of her account of Mexican American life. She recalls countering her editor's disbelief by saying "you would be surprised how little I made up, I had to make up . . . [some of it] is part of the local folklore, the malogra that attacks Caridad in the middle of the night on the crossroads, it's one of these universal terrors at night

that men have reported." See also Castillo's comments in an interview with Bryce Milligan (especially 26).

9. See also María Herrera-Sobek, who argues that Castillo integrates folklore and humor into her political commentary. Thus Herrera-Sobek links M.O.M.A.S. to the Madres de la Plaza de Mayo in Argentina, the women who formed an organization to protest the disappearance of their children during the dirty war ("Folklore" 198).

10. Mary Pat Brady also focuses on the experimentalism in Cisneros's prose fiction and points out the resemblance between her stories and contemporary gay fiction, or, in Ross Chambers's words, 'loiterature' (119–24).

11. In her interview with Dasenbrook and Jussawalla, Cisneros has professed her interest in the poetry of the spoken word: "So . . . I was like a linguist roaming around listening to people. Sometimes I was more concerned with the how than the what of what they said. . . . Being in Texas and listening to how people speak in Texas brought me back to my original love, and that is the rhythm of the spoken word" (291). See also Pratt for a discussion of a tendency in contemporary short stories to embrace orality (189).

12. Significantly, Cisneros has discussed plans to adapt the story into a play (Cisneros, "A Reading").

13. For a discussion of the rival cults of the Virgin of Guadalupe and Nuestra Señora de los Remedios, as well as their relation to Nahua goddesses, see María Herrera-Sobek, especially chapter three (*The Mexican Corrido*).

Chapter 5
Desert Women, **Brujas***, and* **Curanderas***: Pat Mora's Linguistic* **Mestizaje**

1. The only exception is a poem dedicated to her father, "Corazón del corrido" (*Agua Santa* 12–15), written entirely in Spanish. To write it, Mora explains, she had to learn an entirely new form (Mermann-Jozwiak and Sullivan). There is also a short poem in Spanish, "En la Sangre" (*Chants* 44), but it is translated on the same page.

2. See Muriel Saville-Troike. She also explains that an "ethnography of communication takes language first and foremost as a *socially situated* cultural form" (2; emphasis added).

3. In the U.S.-American publishing world, the politics of using foreign words is carefully scripted: they appear in italics. Reed Way Dasenbrook has argued that as a result of historical encounters with Mexico, the Spanish language is not as highly regarded as other European languages such as French or German. When faced with French or German phrases in a text, readers tend to find the writer sophisticated, while Spanish phrases rather evoke incomprehension and unintelligibility. Leticia Garza-Falcón has noted that her book *Gente Decente* was the first one published by the University of Texas Press that had a Spanish/English title (Personal communication with the author).

4. Poet Diana Montejano also speaks of the elaborate system of punishment devised by schools to discourage the use of Spanish (Mermann-Jozwiak and Sullivan 1–2).

5. For similar claims, see Hurtado and Rodríguez (413). See also James F. Tollefson on ELL debates in Texas in 1988, suggesting parallels between the ELL movement to anti-immigration movements of the nineteenth century (130).

6. Of course it is ironic that in these postmodern times, advertisers don't hesitate to use Spanish to sell their products to Latino communities; it is not unusual for salsa to be a common household item; and Spanish-language TV is all over the airwaves.

7. See Savin and Alfred Arteaga for an application of Bakhtinian principles of monologism/dialogism and heteroglossia to code-switching. See also Pat Mora, who states that moving away from the border area means missing "the pleasures of moving back and forth between two languages—a pleasure that can deepen human understanding and *increase our versatility conceptually* as well as linguistically" (*Nepantla* 10; emphasis added).

8. See Carol Myers-Scotton and Gary D. Keller for valuable accounts of the history of debates on code-switching among linguists.

9. See especially Gonzáles's chapter three, "The Politics of Language."

10. But note that Mora shows the *abuela* in a multitude of subject positions, including as cannery worker in "Family Ties" (*Chants* 43), as isolated individual in "Village Therapy" (*Chants* 40), as dozing chaperone in "Letting Go" (*Chants* 56), and as worrying mother figure in "Withdrawal Symptoms" (*Borders* 26–7).

11. On a different note, Ana Castillo has asked her editors to include Spanish phrases "more naturally," i.e. unmarked by italics, into the texts of her novels to more accurately reflect the linguistic experiences of Mexican Americans. I argue that since we are used to the convention of quoting foreign words in italics, not using italics is more disruptive. See also Sonia Saldívar-Hull's statement that she uses interlingualism as a conscious political act (*Feminism* 173, note 1).

12. See my discussion of Gaspar de Alba's "Literary Wetback" in chapter one.

13. Mora's conscious construction of spatial arrangements is evident in her comments on poetry and space. In an interview, she states, "My first love is poetry. I love the white space on the page, love the feeling that I can shape that space in all kinds of ways. Maybe this has to do with the whole interest in space and geography and coming from the desert and having lots of space, and I love that space" (Mermann-Jozwiak and Sullivan).

Conclusion: Decolonizing the Postmodern

1. See Lange-Churión and Mendieta, who similarly argue that "Latin America is not supplemental or external to (Post)modernity. Instead, it is integral to it" (14).

Works Cited

Adams, Kate. "Northamerican Silences: History, Identity, and Witness in the Poetry of Gloria Anzaldúa, Cherríe Moraga, and Leslie Marmon Silko." *Listening to Silences: New Essays in Feminist Criticism.* Ed. Elaine Hedges and Shelley Fisher Fishkin. New York: Oxford UP, 1994. 130–45.

Adams, Noah. "Story of Chicana Family Setting for *So Far From God.*" *All Things Considered National Public Radio.* KEDT, Corpus Christi. 27 May 1993.

Adams, Timothy Dow. "Introduction: Life Writing and Light Writing: Autobiography and Photography." *Modern Fiction Studies* 40 (1994): 459–91.

Alarcón, Antonio V. Menéndez. *Power and Television in Latin America: The Dominican Case.* Westpoint, Conn.: Praeger Press, 1992.

Alarcón, Norma. "Conjugating Subjects: The Heteroglossia of Essence and Resistance." Arteaga 125–138.

——."Interview with Pat Mora." *Third Woman* 3 (1986): 121–126.

——."The Sardonic Powers of the Erotic in the Work of Ana Castillo." Horno-Delgado et al. 94–107.

——."The Theoretical Subject(s) of *This Bridge Called My Back* and Anglo-American Feminism." Anzaldúa, *Making Face* 356–369.

——."Traddutora, Traditora: A Paradigmatic Figure of Chicana Feminism." Grewal and Kaplan 110–33.

Alcott, Louisa May. *Little Women.* Toronto: Bantam, 1983.

Anzaldúa, Gloria. *Borderlands/La Frontera: The New Mestiza.* San Francisco: Spinsters/ Aunt Lute, 1987.

——."Haciendo caras, una entrada." *Making Face* xv–xxviii.

——. ed. Making Face, Making Soul: Haciendo caras. Creative and Critical Perspectives by *Feminists of Color.* San Francisco: Aunt Lute Books, 1990.

Aparicio, Frances R. "On Sub–versive Signifiers: U.S. Latina/o Writers Tropicalize English." *American Literature* 66.4 (1994): 795–901.

Arteaga, Alfred, ed. *An Other Tongue: Nation and Ethnicity in the Linguistic Borderlands.* Durham and London: Duke UP, 1994.

——."An Other Tongue." *An Other Tongue* 9–33.

Ashcroft, Bill, Gareth Griffiths, and Helen Tiffin. *The Empire Writes Back: Theory and Practice in Post-Colonial Literatures.* London: Routledge, 1989.

Athey, Stephanie. "Poisonous Roots and the New World Blues: Rereading Seventies Narration and Nation in Alex Haley and Gayl Jones." *Narrative* 7.2 (1999): 169–93.

Bakhtin, Mikhail M. *The Dialogic Imagination. Four Essays.* Ed. Michael Holquist. Austin: U of Texas P, 1981.

Baro, Madeline. "INS Hoping Potential Agents Make a Run for the Border Patrol." *Corpus Christi Caller Times* 26 Apr. 1998. A15+.

Barr, Marlene S. *Feminist Fabulation: Space/Postmodern Fiction.* Iowa City: U of Iowa P, 1992.

Barth, John. *Lost in the Funhouse.* New York: Anchor Books, 1988.

Barthelme, Frederick. "On Being Wrong: Convicted Minimalist Spills Bean." *New York Times Book Review* 3 Apr. 1988. 1.

Barthes, Roland. *Camera Lucida: Reflections on Photography.* New York: Hill and Wang, 1981.

Batchen, Geoffrey. *Burning with Desire: The Conception of Photography.* Cambridge, Mass.: The MIT Press,

1997.

Belsey, Catherine. *Critical Practice.* London, New York: Methuen, 1980.

Benjamin, Walter. "The Work of Art in the Age of Mechanical Reproduction." *Illuminations: Essays and Reflections.* New York: Schocken Books, 1968. 217–251.

Berger, John. *Ways of Seeing.* London: Penguin Books, 1977.

Bergland, Betty. "Rereading Photographs and Narratives in Ethnic Autobiography: Memory and Subjectivity in Mary Antin's *The Promised Land.*" *Memory, Narrative, and Identity: New Essays in Ethnic American Literatures.* Ed. Amritjit Singh, Joseph T. Skerrett, Jr., andRobert E. Hogan. Boston: Northeastern UP, 1994. 45–88

Bernal, Mary Ann. "Sacrifice and Transformation: Ana Castillo's *So Far From God.*" *Texas College English* 27 (1994–5): 23–27.

Bhabha, Homi. *The Location of Culture.* London and New York: Routledge, 1994.

Blom, Jan, and John J. Gumperz. "Social Meaning in Structure: Code-Switching in Norway." *Directions in Sociolinguistics.* Ed. John J. Gumperz and D. Hymes. New York: Holt, Rinehart, and Winston, 1972. 409–34.

Bourdieu, Pierre. *Photography: A Middle-brow Art.* Stanford: Stanford UP, 1990.

Brady, Mary Pat. "The Contrapuntal Geographies of *Woman Hollering Creek and Other Stories.*" *American Literature* 71 (1999): 117–50.

Bridgewood, Christine. "Family Romances: The Contemporary Popular Family Saga." *The Progress of Romance: The Politics of Popular Fiction.* Ed. Jean Redford. London: Routledge, 1986. 167–93.

Bruce-Novoa, Juan. "A Case of Identity: What's in a Name? Chicanos and Riqueños." *RetroSpace* 33–39.

——.*RetroSpace: Collected Essays on Chicano Literature, Theory, and History.* Houston: Arte Público Press, 1990.

——."Spanish-Language Loyalty and Literature." *RetroSpace* 41–51.

Bürger, Peter. *Theorie der Avantgarde.* Frankfurt a.M.: edition suhrkamp, 1974.

Calderón, Héctor. "The Novel and the Community of Readers: Rereading Tomás Rivera's *Y no se lo tragó la tierra.*" Calderón and Saldívar 97–113.

——."Texas Border Literature: Cultural Transformation and Historical Reflection in the Works of Américo Paredes, Rolando Hinojosa and Gloria Anzaldúa." *Dispositio* 16 (1993): 13–27.

Calderón, Héctor, and José David Saldívar, eds. *Criticism in the Borderlands: Studies in Chicano Literature, Culture, and Ideology.* Durham and London: Duke UP, 1991.

——."Editors' Introduction: Criticism in the Borderlands." Calderón and Saldívar 1–7.

Candelaria, Cordelia Chávez. "*Différance* and the Discourse of 'Community' in Writings by and about the Ethnic Other(s)." Arteaga 185–202.

Cantú, Norma Elía. *Canícula: Snapshots of a Girlhood en la Frontera.* Albuquerque: U of New Mexico P, 1995.

Cardillo, Delfina Silva. "Do You Switch Languages in Mid-Sentence? *No hay que* Apologize." *Vista* 6. 27.3 (1991): 10.

Carr, Robert. "Crossing the First World/Third World Divides: Testimonial, Transnational Feminisms, and the Postmodern Condition." Grewal and Kaplan 153–172.

Castillo, Ana. *So Far From God.* New York: Norton, 1993.

Castillo, Debra A., and María Socorro Tabuenca Córdoba. *Border Women: Writing from la frontera.* Minneapolis: U of Minnesota P, 2002.

Cavazos, Daniel R. "Operation Rio Grande." *Corpus Christi Caller Times* 23 Aug. 1997: A19.

Cervantes, Lorna Dee. "Para un Revolucionario." Rebolledo and Rivero 151–52.

Chabram, Angie. "Conceptualizing Chicano Critical Discourse." Calderón and Saldívar 127–48.

Chabram-Dernersesian, Angie. "I Throw Punches for My Race, But I Don't Want to Be a Man: Writing Us--Chica-nos (Girl, Us)/Chicanas--into the Movement Script." *Cultural Studies.* Ed. Lawrence Grossberg, Cary Nelson, and Paula Treichler. New York, London: Routledge, 1992. 81–96.

Chávez, Denise. "Novena Narrativas y Ofrendas Nuevomexicanas." *Chicana Creativity and Criticism:*

Charting New Frontiers in American Literature. Ed. María Hererra-Sobek and Helena María Viramontes. Houston: Arte Público Press, 1988. 85–100.

Chow, Rey. "Rereading Mandarin Ducks and Butterflies: A Response to the 'Postmodern' Condition." *Cultural Critique* 5 (1986–87): 69–93.

Cisneros, Sandra. *"Bien* Pretty." *Woman* 137–65.

——. *The House on Mango Street*. Houston: Arte Público Press, 1985.

——. "I Can Live Sola and I Love to Work." *La Voz de Esperanza* Mar 1995. 3–6.

——. "Little Miracles, Kept Promises." *Woman* 116–29.

——. "A Reading." Corpus Christi Literary Society. Richardson Auditorium, Del Mar College. 3 February 1995.

——. "Salvador Late or Early." *Woman* 10-11.

——. Woman Hollering Creek and Other Stories. New York: Vintage, 1991.

Cixous, Hélène. "Sorties." *New French Feminisms: An Anthology*. Ed. Elaine Marks and Isabelle de Courtivron. Amherst: U of Massachusetts P, 1980. 90–98.

Clark, Miriam Marty. "Contemporary Short Fiction and the Postmodern Condition." *Studies in Short Fiction* 32 (1995): 147–59.

Clifford, James. "Introduction: Partial Truths." Clifford and Marcus 1–16.

——. "On Ethnographic Allegory." Clifford and Marcus 98–121.

Clifford, James, and George E. Marcus, eds. *Writing Culture: The Poetics and Politics of Ethnography*. Berkeley: U of California P, 1986.

Cohen, Marvin. *The Monday Rhetoric of the Love Club and Other Parables*. New York: New Directions, 1994.

Connor, Steven. *Postmodernist Culture: An Introduction to Theories of the Contemporary*. Oxford: Basil Blackwell, 1989.

Cota-Cárdenas, Margarita. *Marchitas de mayo (sones pa'l pueblo): poesías chicana*. Austin: Relámpago Books Press, 1989.

Cornier Michaels, Magali. *Feminism and the Postmodern Impulse: Post-World War II Fiction*. Albany, NY: State U of New York P, 1996.

Crapanzano, Vincent. "Hermes' Dilemma: The Masking of Subversion in Ethnographic Description." Clifford and Marcus 51–76.

Dasenbrook, Reed Way. "Intelligibility and Meaningfulness in Multicultural Literature." *PMLA 102.1* (1987): 10–19.

Dasenbrook, Reed Way, and Feroza Jussawalla. "Interview with Sandra Cisneros." *Interviews with Writers of the Post-Colonial World*. Jackson: U of Mississippi P, 1992. 286–306.

DeCarlo, Tessa. "Look at the Camera, Smile . . . Got It! A Work of Art!" *The New York Times* Sun., July 5, 1998. 30.

De Crèvecoeur, St. John. "From *Letters from an American Farmer*, 'What Is an American.'" *American Literature Survey*. Ed. Milton R. Stern and Seymour L. Gross. Vol I. New York: Viking, 1975. 332–357.

de Hoyos, Angela. *Arise! Chicano, and Other Poems*. San Antonio: M&A Editions, 1975.

de Lauretis, Teresa, ed. *Feminist Studies/Critical Studies*. Bloomington: Indiana UP, 1986.

——. *Technologies of Gender: Essays on Theory, Film, and Fiction*. Bloomington: U of Indiana P, 1987.

Deleuze, Gilles, and Félix Guattari. *Kafka: Toward a Minor Literature*. Minneapolis: U of Minnesota P, 1986.

——. A Thousand Plateaus. Transl. Brian Massumi. Minneapolis: U of Minnesota P, 1987.

De Valdés, María Elena. "The Critical Reception of Sandra Cisneros's *House on Mango Street*." *Gender, Self, and Society: Proceedings of the IV International Conference on the Hispanic Cultures of the United States*. Ed. Renate von Bardesleben. Frankfurt: Peter Lang, 1990. 287–300.

Derrida, Jacques. "Différance." *Margins of Philosophy*. Transl. Alan Bass. Chicago: U of Chicago P, 1982. 1–28.

——. "Freud and the Scene of Writing." *Writing and Difference*. Transl. Alan Bass. Chicago: U of Chicago P, 1978. 196–232.

——. *Glas.* Transl. John P. Leavey, Jr., and Richard Rand. Lincoln: U of Nebraska P, 1986.

——. "The Law of Genre." *Critical Inquiry* 7 (1980): 55–83.

——. "Living On: BORDER LINES." *Deconstruction and Criticism.* Ed. Harold Bloom et al. New York: Seabury Press, 1979. 75–176.

——. *Margins of Philosophy.* Transl. Alan Bass. Chicago: U of Chicago P, 1982.

——. Positions. Transl. Alan Bass. Chicago: U of Chicago P, 1981.

Dixon, Melvin. *Ride Out the Wilderness: Geography and Identity in Afro-American Literature.* Urbana and Chicago: U of Illinois P, 1987.

Dunn, Timothy J. *The Militarization of the U.S.-Mexico Border 1978–1992: Low-Intensity Conflict Doctrine Comes Home.* Austin: The Center for Mexican American Studies, University of Texas at Austin, 1996.

DuPlessis, Rachel Blau. *Writing beyond the Ending: Narrative Strategies of Twentieth-Century Women Writers.* Bloomington: Indiana UP, 1985.

Durand, Jorge, Douglass S. Massey, and Fernando Charvet. "The Changing Geography of Mexican Immigration in the United States: 1910–1996." *Social Science Quarterly* 81.1 (2000): 1–15.

"El Plan Espiritual de Aztlán." *Aztlán: An Anthology of Mexican American Literature.* Valdez and Steiner 402–3.

Ellison, Ralph. "Stephen Crane and the Mainstream of American Fiction." *Shadow and Act.* New York: New American Library, 1964. 74–88.

Eschbach, Karl, Jacqueline Hagan, and Nestor Rodriguez. *Causes and Trends in Migrant Deaths along the Mexican Border, 1985–1998.* Houston: Center for Immigration Research, 2001. www.uh.edu/cir/causes_andTrends.pdf.

Federman, Raymond. *Double or Nothing: a Real Fictitious Discourse.* Boulder: Fiction Collective Two, 1998.

Fischer, Michael M.J. "Ethnicity and the Post-Modern Arts of Memory." Clifford and Marcus 194–233.

Foster, Hal, ed. *The Anti-Aesthetic: Essays on Postmodern Culture.* Seattle, Wash.: Bay Press, 1983.

——. "Postmodernism: A Preface." *The Anti-Aesthetic* ix–xvi.

Foucault, Michel. *The Order of Things: An Archaeology of the Human Sciences.* New York: Random House, 1973.

——. "Space, Power, and Knowledge." *The Foucault Reader.* Ed. Paul Rabinow. NY: Pantheon Books, 1984. 239–56

Fowlkes, Diane L. "Moving from Feminist Identity Politics to Coalition Politics through a Feminist Materialist Standpoint of Intersubjectivity in Gloria Anzaldúa's *Borderlands/La Frontera: The New Mestiza.*" *Hypatia* 12 (1997): 105–24.

Freedman, Diane P. *An Alchemy of Genres: Cross-Genre Writing by American Feminist Poet-Critics.* Charlottesville: UP of Virginia, 1992.

Friedman, Ellen G., and Miriam Fuchs, eds. *Breaking the Sequence: Women's Experimental Fiction.* Princeton, N.J.: Princeton UP, 1989.

Friedman, Susan Stanford. *Mappings: Feminism and the Cultural Geographies of Encounter.* Princeton, N.J.: Princeton UP, 1998.

Fusco, Coco. "Essential Differences: Photographs of Mexican Women." *English is Broken Here: Notes on Cultural Fusion.* New York: New Press, 1995. 103–12.

Fuss, Diana. *Essentially Speaking: Feminism, Nature, and Difference.* New York: Routledge, 1989.

Galindo, D. Letticia. "Language Use and Language Attitudes: A Study of Border Women." *Bilingual Review/La Revista Bilingüe* 21.1 (1996): 5–17.

Galsworthy, John. *The Forsyte Saga.* New York: Simon and Schuster, 2002.

García, Alma M. "Introduction." *Chicana Feminist Thought: The Basic Historical Writings.* Ed.Alma M. García. New York: Routledge, 1997. 1–18.

García, Ignacio M. *Chicanismo: The Forging of a Militant Ethos Among Mexican Americans.* Albuquerque: U of Arizona P, 1997.

García, Mario T. "*La Frontera:* The Border as Symbol and Reality in Mexican-American Thought."

Between Two Worlds: Mexican Immigrants in the U.S. Ed. David Gutiérrez. Wilmington, Del.: Scholarly Resources, 1996. 89–117.

Garza-Falcón, Leticia M. *Gente Decente: A Borderlands Response to the Rhetoric of Dominance.* Austin: U of Texas P, 1998.

Gaspar de Alba, Alicia. "The Alter-Native Grain: Theorizing Chicano/a Popular Culture." *Culture and Difference: Critical Perspectives on the Bicultural Experience in the United States.* Ed. Antonia Dardner. Westport and London: Bergin & Garvey, 1995. 103–22.

——. "Literary Wetback." *The Massachusetts Review* 29.2 (1988): 242–46. Rpt. in Rebolledo and Rivero 288–292.

Gates, Henry Louis, Jr. "'What's Love Got to Do with It?:' Critical Theory, Integrity, and the Black Idiom." *New Literary History* 18.2 (1987): 345–62.

Gilbert, Fabiola Cabeza de Baca. *The Good Life: New Mexico Traditions and Food.* Santa Fe, N.M.: Museum of New Mexico Press, 1982.

Gitlin, Todd. "Hip-Deep in Post-modernism." *New York Times Book Review* 6 Nov. 1988. 1; 35.

Goldberg, Vicki. "Images of an Economy Devouring the Poor." *New York Times* 22 Mar. 1998, natl. ed., sec.: 44+.

Gómez-Peña, Guillermo. "Documented/Undocumented." *Multicultural Literacy: Opening the American Mind.* Ed. Rick Simonson and Scott Walker. Saint Paul: Graywolf Press, 1988. 127–134.

Gonzales, Rodolfo Corky. "I am Joaquín: Yo soy Joaquín: An Epic Poem." New York, Bantam Books, 1972.

Gonzáles, María. *Contemporary Mexican-American Women Novelists: Towards a Feminist Identity.* New York: Peter Lang, 1996.

Grewal, Inderpal. "Autobiographic Subjects and Diasporic Locations: *Meatless Days* and *Borderlands.*" Grewal and Kaplan, *Scattered Hegemonies* 231–54.

Grewal, Inderpal, and Caren Kaplan. "Introduction: Transnational Feminist Practices and Questions of Postmodernity." Grewal and Kaplan, *Scattered Hegemonies* 1–36.

——. eds. *Scattered Hegemonies: Postmodernity and Transnational Feminist Practices.* Minneapolis: U of Minnesota P, 1994.

Grundberg, Andy. "As It Must to All, Death Comes to Post-Modernism." *New York Times* 16 Sept. 1990. H 52.

Harper, Phillip Brian. *Framing the Margins: The Social Logic of Postmodern Culture.* New York: Oxford UP, 1994.

Harlowe, Barbara. "Sites of Struggle: Immigration, Deportation, Prison, and Exile." Calderón and Saldívar 149–66.

Hassan, Ihab. "Toward a Concept of Postmodernism." *The Postmodern Turn: Essays in Postmodern Theory and Culture.* Columbus: Ohio State UP, 1987. 84–96.

Hedley, Jane. "Nepantilist Poetics: Narrative and Cultural Identity in the Mixed-Language Writings of Irena Klepfisz and Gloria Anzaldúa." *Narrative* 4 (1996): 36–54.

Henderson, Mae. *Borders, Boundaries, and Frames: Essays in Cultural Criticism and Cultural Studies.* New York and London: Routledge, 1995.

Herrera-Sobek, María. *The Mexican Corrido: A Feminist Analysis.* Bloomington: Indiana UP, 1990.

——. "Folklore and Politics and the Construction of Magical Realism in Ana Castillo's Novel *So Far From God.*" Literatura Chicana: Reflexiones y ensayos críticos. Ed. Rosa Morillas Sánchez and Manuel Villar Raso. Granada: Editorial Comares, 2000. 193–201.

Hicks, D. Emily. *Border Writing: The Multidimensional Text.* Minneapolis and Oxford: U of Minnesota P, 1991.

Higonnet, Margaret R. *Borderwork: Feminist Engagements with Comparative Literature.* Ithaca, N.Y.: Cornell UP, 1994.

Hirsch, Marianne. *Family Frames: Narrative Photography and Postmemory.* Cambridge: Harvard UP, 1997.

Hite, Molly. "Postmodern Fiction." *The Columbia History of the American Novel.* Ed. Emory Elliott. New York: Columbia UP, 1991. 697–725.

Hoeveler, J. David Jr. *The Postmodernist Turn: American Thought and Culture in the 1970s.* New York:

Twayne Publishers, 1996.

Hogue, W. Lawrence. *Race, Modernity, Postmodernity: A Look at the History and the Literatures of People of Color Since the 1960s*. Albany: State U of New York P, 1996.

hooks, bell. "Choosing the Margin as a Space of Radical Openness." *Framework* 36 (1989): 15–23.

Horno-Delgado, Asunción, Eliana Ortega, Nina M. Scott, and Nancy Saporta Sternbach, eds. *Breaking Boundaries: Latina Writing and Critical Readings*. Amherst: U of Massachussets P, 1989.

Howe, Irving. "Mass Society and Post-Modern Fiction." *The Idea of the Modern in Literature and the Arts*. New York: Horizon P, 1968. 77–97.

Hurtado, Aída, and Raúl Rodríguez. "Language as a Social Problem: The Repression of Spanish in South Texas." *Journal of Multilingual and Multicultural Development* 10.5 (1989): 401–419.

Hutcheon, Linda. *A Poetics of Postmodernism: History, Theory, Fiction*. New York and London: Routledge, 1988.

——. *The Politics of Postmodernism*. London and New York: Routledge, 1989.

Huyssen, Andreas. "Mapping the Postmodern." *Feminism/Postmodernism*. Ed. Linda J. Nicholson. New York and London: Routledge, 1990. 234–77.

Ikas, Karin. "Interview with Gloria Anzaldúa." *Borderlands/La Frontera: The New Mestiza*. Gloria Anzaldúa. San Francisco: Aunt Lute Books, 2nd ed. 1999. 227–246.

Irigaray, Luce. *This Sex Which Is Not One*. Trans. Catherine Porter with Carolyn Burke. Ithaca: Cornell UP, 1985.

Jackson, David. "'Evasion' Alleged in Border Shooting." *Corpus Christi Caller Times* 14 Aug. 1997: A1+.

Jameson, Fredric. "The Cultural Logic of Late Capitalism." *Postmodernism* 1–54.

——. *The Political Unconscious: Narrative as a Socially Symbolic Act*. Ithaca, NY: Cornell UP, 1981.

——. "Postmodernism and Consumer Society." Foster 111–25.

——. *Postmodernism Or, The Cultural Logic of Late Capitalism*. Durham: Duke UP, 1991.

——. "Theories of the Postmodern." *Postmodernism* 55–66.

Jay, Paul. "The Myth of 'America' and the Politics of Location: Modernity, Border Studies, and the Literature of the Americas." *Arizona Quarterly* 54.2 (1998): 165–192.

Kaplan, Caren. "Deterritorializations: The Rewriting of Home and Exile in Western Feminist Discourse." *Cultural Critique* 6 (1987): 187–98.

——. *Questions of Travel: Postmodern Discourses of Displacement*. Durham and London: Duke UP, 1996.

——. "The Politics of Location as Transnational Feminist Practice." Grewal and Kaplan 137–152.

——. "Reconfigurations of Geography and Historical Narrative: A Review Essay." *Public Culture* 3 (1990): 25–32.

Karl, Frederick R. *American Fictions 1940–1980*. New York: Random, 1985.

Keizer, Arlene. "*Beloved*: Ideologies in Conflict, Improvised Subjects." *African American Review* 33.1 (1999): 105–123.

Keller, Gary D. "The Literary Strategems Available to the Bilingual Chicano Writer." *The Identification and Analysis of Chicano Literature*. Ed. Francisco Jiménez. New York: Bilingual Press, 1979. 263–317.

Kingsolver, Barbara. "Lush Language; Desert Heat; *So Far From God*." *Los Angeles Times Book Review* 16 May 1993. 1.

Kreneck, Thomas H. *Del Pueblo: A Pictoral History of the Houston Hispanic Community*. Houston: Houston International UP, 1989.

Kristeva, Julia. *Revolution in Poetic Language*. Trans. Margaret Waller. New York: Columbia UP, 1984.

La Chrisx. "La Loca de la Raza Cósmica." Rebolledo and Rivero 84.

Lacan, Jacques. "The Mirror Stage as Formative of the Function of the I as Revealed in Psychoanalytic Experience." *Ecrits: A Selection*. New York: Norton, 1977. 1–7.

Lange-Churión, Pedro, and Eduardo Mendieta. *Latin America and Postmodernity: A Contemporary Reader*. Amherst: Humanity Books, 2001.

Lauter, Paul. "Working Class Women's Literature: An Introduction to Study." *Feminisms: An Anthology of Literary Theory and Criticism*. Ed. Robyn R. Warhol and Diane Price Herndl. New Brunswick:

Rutgers UP, 1991. 837–56.

Lawless, Cecilia. "Helena María Viramontes' Homing Devices in *Under the Feet of Jesus.*" *Homemaking: Women Writers and the Politics and Poetics of Home.* Ed. Catherine Wiley and Fiona R. Barnes. New York and London: Garland Publishing, 1996. 361–82.

Limón, José E. *Dancing with the Devil: Society and Cultural Politics in Mexican-American South Texas.* Madison: U of Wisconsin P, 1994.

——. "La llorona, the Third Legend of Greater Mexico: Cultural Sumbols, Women, and the Political Unconscious." *Renato Rosaldo Lecture Series Monograph.* Spr. 1986. Ed. Ignacio M. García. Tucson: U of Arizona P, 1986. 59–93.

Lozano, Elizabeth. "The Force of Myth on Popular Narratives: The Case of Melodramatic Serials." *Communication Theory* 2 (1992): 207–20.

Lugones, María. "On *Borderlands/La Frontera:* An Interpretive Essay." *Hypatia* 7 (1992): 31–37.

——. "Playfulness, 'World'-Travelling, and Loving Perception." Anzaldúa, *Making Face* 390–402.

Lunsford, Andrea A. "Toward a Mestiza Rhetoric: Gloria Anzaldúa on Composition and Postcoloniality." *Race, Rhetoric, and the Postcolonial.* Ed. Gary A. Olson and Lynn Worsham. Albany: State U of New York P, 1999. 43–79.

Lyotard, Jean-François. *The Postmodern Condition: A Report on Knowledge.* Minneapolis: U of Minnesota P, 1984.

Mann, Thomas. *Buddenbrooks: The Decline of a Family.* New York: Vintage Books, 1984.

Márquez, Gabriel García. *One Hundred Years of Solitude.* New York: Bard Books, 1971.

Martin, Biddy, and Chandra Talpade Mohanty. "Feminist Politics: What's Home Got to Do with It?" de Lauretis, *Feminist Studies* 191–212.

Massey, Doreen. *Space, Place, and Gender.* Minneapolis: U of Minnesota P, 1994.

"Massing Border Forces." *Corpus Christi Caller Times* 2 Oct. 1996: B3.

McCracken, Ellen. *New Latina Narrative: The Feminine Space of Postmodern Ethnicity.* Tucson: U of AZ P, 1999.

McHale, Brian. *Constructing Postmodernism.* London, New York: Routledge, 1992.

——. *Pöstmödernist Fiction.* New York and London: Methuen, 1987.

McKenna, Teresa. *Migrant Song: Politics and Process in Contemporary Chicano Literature.* Austin: U of Texas P, 1997.

McRobbie, Angela. *Postmodernism and Popular Culture.* London and New York: Routledge, 1994.

Meese, Elizabeth A. *Crossing the Double Cross: The Practice of Feminist Criticism.* Chapel Hill and London: U of North Carolina P, 1986.

Meier, Matt S. and Feliciano Rivera. *Mexican Americans, American Mexicans: From Conquistadors to Chicanos.* New York: Hill and Wang, 1993.

Mendieta-Lombardo, Eva and Zaida A. Cintron. "Marked and Unmarked Choices of Code Switching in Bilingual Poetry." *Hispana* 78 (1995): 565–571.

Mendoza, Louis. "The Border Between Us: Contact Zone or Battle Zone?" *Modern Fiction Studies* 40 (1994): 119–39.

Mermann-Jozwiak, Elisabeth, and Nancy Sullivan. "Braiding Languages, Weaving Cultures: An Interview with Diana Montejano." Unpublished Manuscript. October 1999.

——. "An Interview with Pat Mora." *MELUS* 28.2 (2003): 139–150.

Michaels, Walter Benn. "Action and Accident: Photography and Writing." *The Gold Standard and the Logic of Naturalism: American Literature at the Turn of the Century.* Berkeley: U of California P, 1987. 215–44.

"Militarization of the U.S.-Mexico Border Would Be A Big Mistake." *Corpus Christi Caller Times* 5 Sept. 2004: A 10.

Miller, Nancy K. "Changing the Subject: Authorship, Writing, and the Reader." de Lauretis, *Feminist Studies* 102–20.

Milligan, Bryce. "An Interview with Ana Castillo." *South Central Review* 16.1 (1999): 19–29.

Mohanty, Chandra Talpade. "Feminist Encounters: Locating the Politics of Experience." *Copyright* 1 (1987): 30–43.

Montejano, David. *Anglos and Mexicans in the Making of Texas, 1836–1986*. Austin: U of Texas P, 1987.

Mora, Pat. *Agua Santa: Holy Water*. Boston: Beacon P, 1995.

——. *Borders*. Houston: Arte Público P, 1986.

——. *Chants*. Houston: Arte Público P, 1984.

——. *Communion*. Houston: Arte Público P, 1991.

——. *Nepantla: Essays from the Land in the Middle*. Albuquerque: U of New Mexico P, 1993.

Moya, Paula M.L. "Chicana Feminism and Postmodern Theory." *Signs* 26 (2001): 441–83.

Myers-Scotton, Carol. *Social Motivations for Codeswitching: Evidence from Africa*. Oxford: Clarendon Press, 1993.

Nancy, Jean Luc. "Cut Throat Sun." Arteaga 113–123.

Nathan, Debbie. "Dangerous Crossings." *In These Times*. 16 Sept. 1996: 12–14.

Neubauer, Carol E. "Developing Ties to the Past: Photography and Other Sources of Information in Maxine Hong Kingston's *China Men*." *MELUS* 10 (1983): 17–36.

Nielsen, Aldon Lynn. *Black Chant: Languages of African-American Postmodernism*. Cambridge: Cambridge UP, 1997.

O'Connell, Jim. "Lawmakers Threaten Border Patrol Funds." *Corpus Christi Caller Times* 27 June 1998: B4.

——. "Sky Eyes to Guard Border." *Corpus Christi Caller Times* 20 Dec. 1997: A1+.

O'Connell, Jim, and Lisa Hoffman. "Pentagon Wants to End Border Duty." *Corpus Christi Caller Times* 15 Jan. 1998: A10+.

"On the Border." *Corpus Christi Caller Times* 15 Mar. 1998: A14.

Olney, James. *Metaphors of the Self: The Meaning of Autobiography*. Princeton: Princeton UP, 1972.

Ortega, Eliana, and Nancy Saporta Sternbach. "At the Threshold of the Unnamed: Latina Discourse in the Eighties." Horno-Delgado et al. 2–23.

Pavletich, JoAnn, and Margot Gayle Backus. "With His Pistol in *Her* Hand: Rearticulating the Corrido Narrative in Helena María Viramontes's 'Neighbors'." *Cultural Critique* (1994): 127–52.

Paz, Octavio. *The Labyrinth of Solitude and Other Writings*. New York: Grove Weidenfeld, 1985.

Pérez, Emma. *The Decolonial Imaginary: Writing Chicanas into History*. Bloomington: U of Indiana P, 1999.

——. *Gulf Dreams*. Berkeley, CA: Third Woman Press, 1996.

Pérez-Torres, Rafael. "Between Presence and Absence: *Beloved*, Postmodernism, and Blackness." *Toni Morrison's Beloved: A Casebook*. Ed. William L. Andrews and Nellie Y. McKay. New York: Oxford UP, 1999. 179–202.

——. "Chicano Ethnicity, Cultural Hybridity, and the Mestizo Voice." *American Literature* 70 (1998): 153–76.

——. *Movements in Chicano Poetry: Against Myths, Against Margins*. Cambridge: Cambridge UP, 1995.

Perry, Donna. *Backtalk: Women Writers Speak Out*. New Brunswick, N.J.: Rutgers UP, 1993.

Poplack, Shana. "Sometimes I'll Start a Sentence in English y termino en español." *Linguistics* 18 (1980): 581–618.

Pratt, Mary Louise. "Fieldwork in Common Places." Clifford and Marcus 27–50.

——. *Imperial Eyes: Travel Writing and Transculturation*. London and New York: Routledge, 1992.

——. "The Short Story: The Long and the Short of It." *Poetics* 10 (1981): 175–94.

Pratt, Minnie Bruce. "Identity: Skin Blood Heart." *Yours in Struggle: Three Feminist Perspectives on Anti-Semitism and Racism*. Ed. Elly Bulkin, Minnie Bruce Pratt, and Barbara Smith. Ithaca, N.Y.: Firebrand Books, 1988. 9–64.

Price-Chalita, Patricia. "Spatial Metaphor and the Politics of Empowerment: Mapping a Place for Feminism and Postmodernism in Geography." *Antipode* 20 (1994): 236–54.

Prodis, Julia. "Border Tragedy Played Out in Flooded Pipe." *Corpus Christi Caller Times* 16 Nov. 1997: A1+.

Quintana, Alvina. *Home Girls: Chicana Literary Voices*. Philadelphia: Temple UP, 1996.

——. "Politics, Representation and the Emergence of a Chicana Aesthetic." *Cultural Studies* 4 (1990):

257–63.

Quiroz, Rudolph Anthony. "Claiming Citizenship: Class and Consensus in a Twentieth-Century Mexican American Community." Diss. U of Iowa, 1998.

Raum, Tom. "House Backs Military Patrols of U.S. Borders." *Corpus Christi Caller Times* 22 May 1998: B 6.

Rebolledo, Tey Diana. "Tradition and Mythology: Signatures of Landscape in Chicana Literature." *The Desert Is No Lady.* Ed. Vera Norwood and Janice Monk. New Haven and London: Yale UP, 1987. 96–124.

——. *Women Singing in the Snow. A Cultural Analysis of Chicana Literature.* Tucson: U of Arizona P, 1995.

Rebolledo, Tey Diana, and Eliana S. Rivero. *Infinite Divisions: An Anthology of Chicana Literature.* Tucson and London: U of Arizona P, 1993.

——. "Introduction." *Infinite Divisions* 1–33.

Reed, Ishmael. *Mumbo Jumbo.* New York: Avon Books, 1970.

Reid, Robert L. *Picturing Texas: The FSA-OWI Photographers in the Lone Star State, 1935–1943.* Austin: Texas State Historical Society, 1994.

Rendón, Armando B. *Chicano Manifesto.* New York: Macmillan, 1972.

Richard, Nelly. "Postmodernism and Periphery." *Third Text* 2 (1987–88): 5–12.

Rivera, Tomás, and Vigil-Piñón, Evangelina. *Y no se lo tragó la tierra.* Houston: Arte Público Press, 1987.

Rocco, Raymond. "The Theoretical Construction of the 'Other' in Postmodernism Thought: Latinos in the New Urban Political Economy." *Cultural Studies* 4 (1990): 321–30.

Roof, Maria. "Maryse Conde and Isable Allende: Family Saga Novels." *World Literature Today* 70 (1996): 283–88.

Rosaldo, Renato. "From the Door of His Tent: The Fieldworker and the Inquisitor." Clifford and Marcus 77–97.

——. "Fables of the Fallen Guy." Calderón and Saldívar 84–93.

——. "Politics, Patriarchs, and Laughter." *Cultural Critique* 6 (1987): 65–86.

Rose, Gillian. *Feminism and Geography: The Limits of Geographical Knowledge.* Minneapolis: U of Minnesota P, 1993.

Rouse, Roger. "Mexican Migration and the Social Space of Postmodernism." *Diaspora: A Journal of Transnational Studies* 1 (1991): 8–23.

"Run From the Border." *Corpus Christi Caller Times* 18 Jan. 1998: A15.

Russell, Charles, ed. *The Avant–Garde Today: An International Anthology.* Urbana: U of Illinois P, 1981.

Sáenz, Benjamin Alire. "Exile, El Paso, Texas." *The Late Great Mexican Border: Reports from a Disappearing Line.* Ed. Bobby Byrd and Susannah Mississippi Byrd. El Paso: Cino Puntos Press, 1996. 199–210.

Saeta, Elsa. "An Interview with Ana Castillo." *Texas College English* 27 (1995): 17–22.

——. "A MELUS Interview: Ana Castillo." *MELUS* 22 (1997): 133–49.

Saldívar, José David. *Border Matters: Remapping American Cultural Studies.* Berkeley: U of California P, 1997.

——. "The Limits of Cultural Studies." *American Literary History* 2 (1990): 251–66.

Saldívar, Ramon. *Chicano Narrative: The Dialectics of Difference.* Madison: U of Wisconsin P, 1990.

Saldívar-Hull, Sonia. "Feminism on the Border: From Gender Politics to Geopolitics." Calderón and Saldívar 203–220.

——. *Feminism on the Border: Chicana Gender Politics and Literature.* Berkeley: U of California P, 2000.

——. "Women Hollering Transfronteriza Feminisms." *Cultural Studies* 13.2 (1999): 251–62.

Sánchez, Marta Ester. *Contemporary Chicana Poetry: A Critical Approach to an Emerging Literature.* Berkeley: U of California P, 1985.

Sánchez, Rosaura. "Postmodernism and Chicano Literature." *Aztlán* 18 (1987): 1–14.

——. *Chicano Discourse: Socio-Historic Perspectives.* Rowley, Mass: Newbury House Publishers, 1983.

Sánchez, Rosaura, and Beatrice Pita. "Mapping Cultural/Political Debates in Latin American Studies." *Cultural Studies* 13.2 (1999): 290–318.

Sandoval, Chela. "U.S. Third World Feminism: The Theory and Method of Oppositional Consciousness in the Postmodern World." *Genders* 10 (1991): 1–24.

Sapir, Michael. "The Impossible Photograph: Hippolyte Bayard's Self-Portrait as a Drowned Man." *Modern Fiction Studies* 40.3 (1994): 619–30.

Saville-Troike, Muriel. *The Ethnography of Communication: An Introduction.* Oxford and Cambridge: Basil Blackwell P, 1993.

Savin, Ada. "Bilingualism and Dialogism: Another Reading of Lorna Dee Cervantes' Poetry." Arteaga 215–24.

Schiller, Dane. "More Force is Urged at Border." *Corpus Christi Caller Times* 6 Dec. 1997: A1+.

Schodolski, Vincent J. "Increased Border Surveillance Keeping Illegal Immigrants in the U.S." *Corpus Christi Caller Times* 2 Nov. 1997: A28.

Simpson, J.A., and E.S.C. Weiner. *The Oxford English Dictionary.* 2nd ed. Vol. XIX. Oxford: Clarendon Press, 1989.

Smith, Sidonie. "Re-citing, Re-siting, and Re-sighting Likeness: Reading the Family Archive in Drucilla Modjeska's *Poppy,* Donna Williams' *Nobody Nowhere,* and Sally Morgan's *My Place.*" *Modern Fiction Studies* 40.3 (1994): 509–43.

Sontag, Susan. *On Photorahy.* New York: Farrar, Strauss and Giroux, 1973.

Spivak, Gayatri Chakravorty. "Subaltern Studies: Deconstructing Historiography." *In Other Worlds: Essays in Cultural Politics.* New York and London: Routledge 1988. 197–221.

Stoddard, Ellwyn R. "Overview." *Borderlands Sourcebook: A Guide to the Literature on Northern Mexico and the American Southwest.* Ed. Richard L. Nostrand Stoddard and Jonathan P. West. Norman: U of Oklahoma P, 1983. 3–5.

Sullivan, Nancy, and Robert T. Schatz. "When Cultures Collide: The Official Language Debate." *Language and Communication* 19 (1999): 261–275.

Swales, Martin B. *Buddenbrooks: Family Life as Mirror of Social Change.* Boston: Twayne, 1991.

Tafolla, Carmen. "Los Corts/Five Voices." *Five Poets of Aztlán.* Ed. Santiago Daydí-Tolson. Binghamton, N.Y.: Bilingual Press/Editorial Bilingüe, 1985. 176–9.

Tagg, John. *The Burden of Representation: Essays on Photographies and Histories.* London: Macmillan Education, 1988.

Thiher, Alan. *Words in Reflection: Modern Language Theory and Postmodern Fiction.* Chicago and London: U of Chicago P, 1984.

Tollefson, James W., ed. *Power and Inequality in Language Education.* Cambridge and New York: Cambridge UP, 1995.

Trachtenberg, Alan. *Reading American Photographs: Images as History. Mathew Brady to Walker Evans.* New York: Hill and Wang, 1989.

Turner, Frederick Jackson. *The Turner Thesis; Concerning the Role of the Frontier in American History.* Ed. George Rogers Taylor. Lexington, Mass.: Heath Publishers, 1971.

Valdez, Luis, and Stan Steiner, eds. *Aztlán: An Anthology of Mexican American Literature.* New York: Alfred A. Knopf, 1972.

Verhovek, Sam Howe. "Mexican Border Fence Friendlier Than a Wall." *New York Times* 8 Dec. 1997, natl. ed.: A1+.

——. "'Silent Deaths' Climbing Steadily as Migrants Cross the Border." *New York Times* 24 Aug. 1997, natl. ed.: A1+.

Villa, Raúl Homero. *Barrio-Logos: Space and Place In Urban Chicano Literature and Culture.* Austin: U of Texas P, 2000.

Viramontes, Helena María. "Tears on My Pillow." *New Chicano/Chicana Writing.* Ed. Charles M. Tatum. Tucson and London: U of Arizona P, 1992.

——. *Under the Feet of Jesus.* New York: Plume, 1996.

Wallace, Michelle. "The Politics of Location: Cinema/Theory/Literature/Ethnicity/ Sexuality/ Me." *Framework* 36 (1989): 42–55.

Waugh, Patricia. *Feminine Fictions: Revisiting the Postmodern.* London and New York: Routledge, 1989.

Ween, Lori. "Family Sagas of the Americas: *Los Sangurimas* and *A Thousand Acres.*" *The Comparatist* 20

(1996): 111–25.

Weiner, Tim. "Bush and Fox Hope Nations Will Become Better Amigos." *New York Times* 31 Jan. 2001, A13.

White, Hayden. *Tropics of Discourse: Essays in Cultural Criticism.* Baltimore and London: The Johns Hopkins UP, 1978.

Woods, Tim. *Beginning Postmodernism.* Manchester and New York: Manchester UP, 1999.

Wyatt, Jean. "On Not Being La Malinche: Border Negotiations of Gender in Sandra Cisneros's 'Never Marry a Mexican' and 'Woman Hollering Creek.'" *Tulsa Studies in Women's Literature* 14 (1995): 243–73.

Yarbro-Bejarano, Yvonne. "Gloria Anzaldúa's *Borderlands/La frontera:* Cultural Studies, 'Difference', and the Non-Unitary Subject." *Cultural Critique* 28 (1994): 5–28.

——. "The Multiple Subject in the Writing of Ana Castillo." *The Americas Review* 20 (1992): 65–72.

Yardley, Jim. "A River That United Lives Is Now a Barrier." *New York Times* 1 Aug. 2002, A1+.

York, Lorraine M. "'The Things That Are Seen in the Flashes': Timothy Findlay's *Inside Memory* as Photographic Life Writing." *Modern Fiction Studies* 40 (1994): 643–56.

Zentella, Ana Celia. "The Hispanophobia of the Official English Movement in the US." International Journal of the Sociology of Language 127 (1997): 71–86.

Index